Not MEANT to BE

TRUSTING GOD FOR THE *Redemption* OF SINGLENESS

JOANNE HOFMEISTER

INK WELL
LITERARY PRESS

INKWELL
LITERARY PRESS

Published by: Inkwell Literary Press, Nashville, TN

ISBN (Print): 978-0-692-07259-2 (E-book): 978-0-692-07260-8

Cover design by: Sarah Siegand
Interior design by: Sarah Siegand
Cover Photography by: Julia Sudnitskaya
Headshot Photography by: Daniel Vertay

To

Sheryl Cook, who understands—

thank you for listening, being the first to read my manuscript, and living a life rich with redemption

and to every beautiful daughter of God

trusting Him to bring her a husband

TABLE OF CONTENTS

"But, Lizzy, I would wish . . .
I should so much *like* . . . to marry for love."

- Jane Bennett in *Pride and Prejudice*[1]

Introduction

For this we have Jesus

I wrote the final version of this book during my fortieth year. Just after my forty-first birthday, right before I picked up the manuscript from my editor, I had my first date with the man who became my husband.

But as I finished this book, I didn't know that date was going to happen. I didn't know marriage was waiting in the wings. At that time, I couldn't understand why I had been waiting for marriage for so long. When I was a child and a teenager, marriage and motherhood were always represented as the normal progression of life for a girl fairly soon after high school or college graduation. This circumstance—goal, even—was especially upheld and valued in Christian communities since marriage and its fruit of children was instituted by God. I grew up in a Christian family, attended church twice every Sunday and on Wednesday nights, and went to a Christian school. My logical expectation and desire was to grow up, get married (ideally in my twenties), and have children.

And so, my reality of "still single at forty" felt like the thing that was "not meant to be."

I never believed, however, that being single meant I was "out of God's will" in the sense of being disobedient to His Word. I thought my job was to wait, and His was to act. I never thought that God disapproved of me because of my marital status. Rather, I expected Him to fulfill what I thought was His vision for my life. As the years went by and that vision didn't come to pass, I grew, at first, discouraged. I sought God and His Word for answers. When I turned forty, discouragement deepened into a dark disappointment, and I sought the help of Christian counselors in my desire for answers.

I needed to understand. I needed to know how to think about my singleness, God's design of marriage and family, and what I should realistically expect for my future.

This is the story of my quest for understanding, and the truth of God that lighted the way.

I am single and disappointed.

Sometimes, I wonder if I'm the only one who feels this way. Single Christian women generally don't talk openly about being disappointed with their singleness. Many of them appear to be filled with faith, waiting on God's timing. I often hear of women being "content while contending in prayer for marriage," believing the day will come when a man will walk through the doorway of their lives, and the rest will be history.

As yet, there isn't that history for me and many of my friends, my never-married friends, and even some long-time divorced friends and acquaintances. All waiting and waiting. I'm waiting with them. How I have longed, and dreamed, and anticipated. I have hoped and believed.

I have expected love.

Love from a godly man, and yes, maybe good-looking, too; a special prince of a man, honored and respected, doing the work of God's kingdom. I expected him to come in the years when men typically come, in the days of youth and beauty, when women flower and ovulate and bounce into motherhood with vigor.

But he hasn't come.

Maybe it's just not meant to be.

Yet, I thought marriage was God's intention. I thought this is why He created Woman, partly—to be the helper of Man. To be his glory and crown, loved and protected, supporting, strengthening, and beautifying his life. Like pillars sculpted in palace style, to which the daughters of Jerusalem were compared—graceful and majestic (Psalm 144:12). Like the pillars of Solomon's temple, named *Jachin* and *Boaz—established* and *strong*, through a deep relationship with the Lord (2 Chronicles 3:17).

Oh, I wanted to be that ornate pillar to his temple.

Beautiful, yet functional. Blessing and contributing and helping the way only a woman can. I thought this was why God gave us this desire for relationship, for nurturing—to be the heart of a family, as my mother was. To make a home. To raise children to also go out and bring God's light to the world. To be part of His plan for changing society and modeling His ways through godly families.

I thought that was God's intention. And I still believe that it is.

That's why to me, it is prolonged singleness that's *not meant to be*. As a human being, I was designed for the partnership of marriage. As a woman, I was fashioned to bear children. As a follower of Christ, I thought marriage and motherhood were a part of God's plan for my life.

For years the conflict has been building: God's intention and my experience. My faith and reality never touching, like train tracks vanishing into the horizon of someday, someday, where they will merge together into fulfillment. Yet, every time the someday seems to have arrived, the tracks are still as far apart as they ever were.

And the horizon seems just as far away as it ever was.

I spoke to a 49-year-old, never-married woman from Canada about this disappointment, its reality. About whether others really feel it as well. "I think it's people not being honest," she said. "They are either fearful of letting God clean out their closet because it's all going to come cascading out, or they are just choosing not to go to that place."

I like her closet analogy. While I know not all unmarried women are disappointed or fearful (I don't like to make total generalizations), I think she's right. I suspect there are many closed closets ready to burst, many rugs thrown over broken hearts.

I think so, because I don't want to go there myself.

I don't want to peel back the layers of my heart and see what's there, to open the closet door and know what falls out. I don't want to look under the bed or the rug, or investigate the cobwebs in the basement.

Somehow, though, deep and lasting disappointment that gathers length and shadow with the passing of time has a way of making itself hard to overlook. Making it hard to hold the door shut, to keep the carpet down. To overlook the cobwebs or the dust bunnies as they spill out from beneath the bed.

In the darkness one longs for light.

But when the light comes, there's nowhere to hide.

I turned forty this year, and the doors finally broke off their hinges. Forty, with its new little roll of belly fat. With its diminishing bloom at the half-point of life, the prime past, the ovulation less plentiful, and the single men like hidden treasure. I am not a wife and don't know if I will ever become a mother. Other dreams about my life's work and calling have not come true. And my mother, to whom I was very close, has recently died. I did not look forward to my fortieth birthday.

I suppose grief and disappointment serve at least one purpose—to make us long for the light more than the external doors and carpets and beds behind and under which our hearts take cover. Eventually, the weight of the stones in our hearts, whatever their cause, drag us down until we can hide them no longer.

And this is how I arrived at forty: legs buckling, ankles turning, tears no longer stuffed behind the shutters of my eyes.

I reached for help outside myself, the decision having been confirmed by Scripture: "You will show me the path of life; in your presence is fullness of joy" (Psalm 16:11, NKJV). Now, I step onto that path and sit from time to time with a woman named Lisa, who listens as everything gushes out.

And the Holy Spirit speaks. He flips on the lights, and I wince at the brightness. I lay everything out to be seen and examined, not by myself in the corners of the basement, but with an honest Christian woman in a comfortable room upstairs in a little house with musty old wooden floors, a place that feels like home. A place that feels safe.

Yet, the Spirit speaks before this. Speaks after this. Speaks in my morning reading of the Word. Through the pastor, the small group, the radio, the worship songs. His voice tumbles toward me at every turn. Flashes of light, like circles from a flashlight or patches of sunshine through leafy tree branches, illuminate something I need to see. His golden threads of light string one feeling to the next, tying together experiences and thoughts, connecting the hidden alcoves and corners of my soul until I start to see clearly. Until I begin to grasp each golden cord and follow it from place to place, untangling what has been, for who knows how long, a dark, heavy mass. Because a life of disappointment is not God's intention, either.

The Spirit of life and truth, of peace and comfort, is always whispering, singing, painting through flowers and clouds and the colors of sunlight, speaking through men's voices and women's voices and black-and-white words, speaking in His own still, small voice of Christ, the living Word.

Christ, the Redeemer—that name of His I love most. Without Him, there would be no light, no places for hearts to mend and heal, to unwind and untangle the darkness and falsehoods that flood it with disappointment's black ink—even when it's about long-lasting singleness. Yes, even for that unspoken grief, so often seemingly unacceptable to the rest of the (married) Church, there is grace. As my mother would say, quoting the words on a little plaque she read often when the cancer returned: *For this I have Jesus.*

We have Emmanuel; we have Redeemer. The one who ransomed us from sin's cursed punishment by taking it Himself. The one who rescued us from eternal death. The one whose resurrection makes us a new creation, even while we are here on this fallen earth.

It is this Redeemer, holding incomprehensible capacity for redemption, that speaks to me about prolonged singleness and disappointment and dreams unfulfilled. He speaks about His heart for me and all His daughters who share my experience.

And so, as I walk forward on the path of life, I write. Honestly and openly. I write as I look inside. I write as I open the door and let out what will come, whether it crashes and breaks or simply floats in the aftermath like feathers from a pillow.

The resulting pages chronicle my inner journey through prolonged singleness. I start with the conflict in my heart, the truth that God created women, including me, for marriage, and the reality that many of the women in my generation, including me, are not married. Beautiful, Christian women, none of us perfect, but all of us seeking to follow God and His plan for our lives. Expecting that marriage would and should be part of that plan, for good reason. Waiting with hope toward the edges of our childbearing years, wondering what waits for us on the other side.

I travel through deep and honest channels of my heart: Is prolonged singleness God's plan or punishment? Our fault or His gift? What do today's singleness and marriage trends have to do with my singleness, and with yours? I peer through the lenses of sovereignty and circumstance, of expectation and disappointment, trying to make it all fit. Trying to find the answers, to know and understand the God I love in the middle of it.

And I do find Him. I find His heart, the one named Love. The heart that bled redemption and lives redemption still. And that heart is really the only answer I need. Because from that heart flows the goodness and work of redemption in my life, even when it comes to singleness.

Because *for this we have Jesus.* He knows our feelings, desires, and losses; and He wants to do something with them. He offers His love and predestined purpose, not as vague ideas but as specific life-giving experiences in our lives. He offers restored joy and fulfillment and anticipation.

And this is what I love writing about most: redemption. The redemption of singleness. *My* singleness. *Your* singleness. What it is, what it looks like, why we can expect it.

So thank you for being bold enough and interested enough to come into the pages of my heart. I hope you read them with respect and care as you wear my heart on your sleeve.

But even more, I hope you leave with a little something to take with you on your own journey—an encouragement, an insight, a breakthrough. Maybe even just one fitly spoken word, your own golden apple set in silver as a gift from the Holy Spirit (Proverbs 25:11).

And maybe that word will be *hope.*

NOTES

1. Andrew Davies, *Pride and Prejudice*, The Special Edition, Volume 1, directed by Simon Langton, aired September 1995 (A&E home video, 2001), DVD.

Part 1

Not Meant to be

"One of the trials of woman-kind is the fear of being an old maid."

- Louisa May Alcott

– Chapter 1 –

Old Maid or Specially Gifted?

"You girls aren't going to be old maids, are you?"

The question rushed at me like an assailant.

Not if I can help it, I thought. But could I help it? Was meeting the right man and getting married something I could control?

My sister and I, both in our early thirties at the time, were visiting elderly friends of our grandparents. We hadn't seen them in years, and of course they were curious to know if we had any marriage prospects.

We didn't.

Hence, the question about becoming old maids. In the following conversation, it became apparent that this couple thought we were headed in that direction. Completely at risk.

Old maid. Immediately, I picture poor Mary in *It's a Wonderful Life*, whose fate is to become a bespectacled, unmarried librarian when her husband, George Bailey, experiences the world as if he had never been born. (A side note: Clarence the angel, who grants George this wish, calls Mary an old maid, though at this point in the story she wouldn't yet have been forty years old. A second side note: She hadn't worn glasses as a married woman.)

I remember something from my childhood: a sketch of an old maid that featured a witch-like woman with stringy hair, scowling eyes and a bulging, stubbly chin (all she missed was the glasses). As kids, my sisters and I played the Old Maid card game. While the lady on the Old Maid card wasn't ugly, she did look sad, knitting away in her lonely rocking chair. The message of the game was clear: The goal was *not* to end up with that card.

Certainly this elderly couple, heralding the warning that we were about to become old maids, didn't mean to be unkind. And yet, I recall these images. Not to mention the dictionary description: *spinster, mildly disparaging.*

Spinster, that antiquated word, identified single, working women as far back as the seventeenth century, but it did not originally have negative connotations. Over time, and particularly in England, it became associated with the unpleasant and ugly single woman, that antiquated maiden herself.[1] The negativity has never quite worn off.

A friend explained to me that in the young days of my grandparents' generation, a woman was thought to remain unmarried if she were tight-fisted, miserly and miserable, a woman in whose eyes no man would ever measure up. A woman no man would want to be with anyway, like a mean librarian who frowns at giggling children. Old maid, then. A woman's recompense for being too picky, unattractive and otherwise disqualified for marriage.

To my elderly friends, it was at the very least incomprehensible that two women approaching their mid-thirties would not yet be married. I'm sure they didn't think we were unworthy or unattractive. Maybe, though, they secretly wondered what our problem was. We were past due for marriage—especially me, the husband inferred, because I am older than my sister. Which feels especially disparaging.

The truth is, I've often felt that way myself: *past due for marriage*. I never thought I would be single at thirty, let alone forty. Maybe it *is* my fault, and the disappointment simply comes with the territory.

IT'S NOT JUST ME

Yet, these words: "There's no reason why a woman like you should have trouble getting married."

Ah, thank you, kind gentleman around my father's age. He told me this in the fall of my thirty-ninth year. (I was secretly hoping his handsome son would ask me out, but that's another story.)

Thing is, I'm not the only one "having trouble" getting married. In case anyone hasn't noticed, "young couples" are older than they used to be. Our society in general is increasingly "less married." Something's been up for a while now, building into a long crescendo over the years. And I can hear it loud and clear. Consider some recent statistics: "The median age at first marriage increased to 28.2 for men and 26.[1] for women in 2010, an increase from 26.8 and 25.1 in 2000, according to the U.S. Census Bureau. This increase is a continuation of a long-term trend that has been noted since the mid-1950s. In addition, the overall percentage of adults who were married declined to 54.1 percent in 2010 from 57.3 percent in 2000."[2]

My trouble, it seems, is much worse than the statistics suggest, since I'm long past 26.1 years of age. But I've been trying to understand my singleness since I was at least that age.

If this is my fault, then there are a whole lot of other flawed women who must bear the old maid responsibility with me, those of us quickly reaching and surpassing Mary Bailey's under-forty-years-old stint at the library in George's nonexistence. I mean particularly the women of Generation X, my generation, born between the mid-1960s and 1980. In her well-researched book, *Where Have All the Good Men Gone?*, A.J. Keisling speaks of us as the "lost girls":

"There exists a vast undiscovered population of single women (in this case, specifically Christian women) whom marriage seemingly sidestepped or at least put on hold for an indefinite period of time. In many ways it seems these women are truly lost in time, set apart from the generations that have gone before them."[3]

We aren't like the women of the generation before us, like my seventeen-year-old mother who married right out of high school: a post-war generation booming forward with life. We aren't like the generation following us, at least like the ones in my church. It's their weddings, for the most part, I've attended over the last several years. Many of them already have kids. They are the Generation Next, inventive children of the Millennium.

And in between are the Xers, branded by the world as generic and lacking identity, the unknowns in uncertain times.[4] Of course, many people in my generation are married. But many are not—we are significantly less married than any previous generation. For me, year after year, wedding after wedding, it's difficult not to feel like forgotten, faux pearl beads lost between the cushions of the couch while the diamonds of the Millennial Generation crown the heads of dashing young princes on the ballroom floor.

As these brides who seem so young transition from *single* to *married*, and later, to *mother*, it's challenging not to feel like *old maid.*

It's challenging to know how to respond to my generation's singleness at all, a circumstance that feels like it wasn't meant to be.

We are followers of Christ who lead and serve in various ministries. We are attractive and talented, created by God and marked as His chosen generation. We are called to light and life and praise. In Him, we are not the black smudge of an *X* at the bottom of a form that someone else signs.

Yet, many of us are women who don't have boyfriends or lots of dates. Many of us are never-married, some single again, for a very long time. We sit at church (without the stringy hair and jutting chins, I might add), worshipping, listening, growing, and waiting. Wondering if the seat next to us will ever be occupied with a spouse, if the call on our lives will ever come to fruition with a life partner. Are all of us really that bad?

MAYBE THEY'RE RIGHT

Soon after making the "old maid" comment, my elderly friends were quick to point out that some people have "the gift of singleness."

Oh no, here we go, saving face.

If it's not really my fault, then it must be my gift.

But maybe they are right. Maybe I, my sister, my friends, my acquaintances and hundreds of other Christian women across North America all have "the gift of singleness," as Paul spoke of it in 1 Corinthians 7.

I doubt it.

Paul seemed to speak of this gift as a conviction to voluntarily refrain from marriage, at least for a season, for the purpose of serving the Lord. But today's trend of prolonged singleness is not typically included on the receiver's wish list. I don't think my generation's experience is exactly what Paul was talking about.

All of us need God's revelation to help us see how any challenging season of our lives—be it one of singleness, marriage, child rearing, grief, loss, or prolonged waiting—is a gift with very unique opportunities to know and trust Him. In that sense, singleness is a gift that should be used to devote oneself to Him, as Paul instructed.

But Paul and Jesus both said that choosing singleness, which also means choosing celibacy, is not desirable or acceptable for everyone (Matthew 19:11-12). What then, if singleness is not voluntary, yet marriage doesn't come? Does it mean we've done something to forfeit the privilege and biblical design to be part of a marriage that glorifies God?

Maybe singleness *is* the fault of the single woman. For some of us, at least some of the time, it certainly could be—no, probably is. Maybe we've allowed past hurt to jade our view of men, or we judge and criticize them before giving them a chance. Perhaps we are looking for a man who's perfect, even if we don't think (or admit) we are. Maybe we are so afraid that we end up chasing men away, before they can reject us. Maybe God is allowing us to grow, heal, and mature before we meet our husbands.

I am so grateful for the work He's done in my life as a single woman. I don't want to know what would have happened if I had gotten married right out of college. I hardly knew who I was, let alone who I was in Christ. My unresolved emotion and immaturity would have led to an unpleasant marriage, at least initially.

Oh, that poor guy. I would have been like Jacob, as described by Dr. Timothy Keller:

> If you get married as Jacob did, putting the weight of all your deepest hopes and longings on the person you are marrying, you are going to crush him or her with your expectations… No person, not even the best one, can give your soul all it needs. You are going to think you have gone to bed with Rachel, and you will get up and it will always be Leah. This cosmic disappointment and disillusionment is there in all of life, but we especially feel it in the things upon which we most set our hopes.[5]

If we expect a husband to be our everything—our life, our identity, our idol, our hope—then we'd better pray God convicts and changes us during our season of singleness.

Perhaps we've worked through some major issues in our lives and are grateful to be in a more mature place now than we once were. What else is God expecting from us before He brings along that man? Is He waiting for us to meet that goal weight, begin a new ministry, or attain a certain level of holiness?

Sometimes, one gets that impression. But I don't think it's from God. Writer Debbie Maken explains well what often happens inside the Church:

> "God is your husband." "Bloom where you are planted." "There are plenty of ministries you can help with during this time." "Be content." "Make the desire of your heart Jesus, not marriage." The desire for marriage has been placed on a collision course

> with the desire for God, the One Who made marriage in the first place. With this kind of pitting, singles are often reduced to extolling singleness, much like a witch having the grace to drown to prove innocence.[6]

Does my disappointment in this unfulfilled desire mean I don't desire or love God enough? While it does mean that I've had to continue surrendering the desire for marriage, and my own timeline for it, to Him, it doesn't negate my love for Him. I don't want to love God with any strings attached; I am committed to living for Him even if I never get married. Yet, I still long to have a life partner. Sometimes, I ache for one. (Am I allowed to say that out loud?)

Focusing on Jesus and living contentedly with His love are God's requirements for everyone. They are not the unique responsibility of the unmarried. A love relationship with God should—it must—take precedence over any other relationship and desire of our hearts. It is what fulfills the human soul, married or single. It empowers a devoted life of singleness and enables a God-centered marriage to portray God's character and heart for intimate relationship with His people.

Author Lori Smith says that in the Bible, "Marriage is never equated with having attained a sufficient level of spiritual growth, and singleness is never deprecated as the school of instruction for those who just don't get the Christian life. Both are presented as mature alternatives for the spiritual Christian."[7]

Dr. Keller provides some context for this conclusion, explaining how radical a single life would have been to people in

Paul's time. People were not single unless they were prostitutes. All social status, security, personal significance and future hope in ancient societies revolved around the family, making marriage and having children one's most important goals. Paul's words about choosing to remain single were revolutionary.

"Christianity is the first tradition that ever lifted up long-term singleness as an adult and said, 'This is a perfectly good way to be,'" Keller says, because an individual's identity, significance, and security are all found in Christ. Keller, speaking on 1 Corinthians 6 and 7, was saying, in essence, "God, not your marital status, defines your life" (1 Corinthians 7:17, *The Message*).[8]

Every child of God, married or single, is made complete in Christ. Identified. Named. *Sought Out* and *Not Forsaken*, as Isaiah 62 puts it. But being complete in Christ does not eradicate the desire for marriage, nor its design.

God created Woman in the context of marriage. The desire for intimate partnership is a seed embedded in her heart, taken from Man's. God planted it there in Eden when Adam slept his deep sleep and God took one of his bones to shape his wife. Woman was fashioned from Man, and there is a deep part of her that longs to return to him, to belong to him once more as bone of his bone and flesh of his flesh, in the biblical "one flesh" definition of marriage.

So, no. The "vast undiscovered population of single women" in the Church are not undeserving old maids. Nor are we "specially gifted" with singleness over the rest of the married population.

THE UNANSWERED QUESTION

It is a Saturday morning several years after the old maid incident. I enter a bookstore café for a day of writing. The place is packed and I snag the only empty seat, one of two armchairs with a small table between them. The other armchair is occupied by a man with gleaming blue eyes. A man from my generation.

Who is not wearing a wedding band.

I sit down with my tea and unpack my laptop. I glance sideways. *There's no way that guy would happen to be a Christian. But even if he were, what are the odds that he would speak to me?*

The odds, it turns out, are one hundred percent. He's very friendly. He starts a conversation. He has a foreign accent. And he happens to be a Christian.

Forty-five minutes and a new Facebook friend later, I'm in a bit of shock. I get into my writing; he works on his project.

Much later, I return to my car and suddenly remember my cynical mental monologue when I spotted the man at the bookstore. Earlier that morning I had been thinking about singleness, the fault or the gift, the still-unanswered question of *why*. And the seemingly impossible feat of meeting an older, unmarried Christian man.

The Lord had more work to do on that cynicism and negativity, things that surely do not attract single men to single women. But that day, I marveled with thanksgiving at the divinely orchestrated intersection of man and woman, at God's direct answer to my complaint that such encounters seemed rare and impossible.

God reminded me that with Him, all things are possible. But why do those encounters *feel* impossible? I had more investigating to do, more questions to ask about what else could be contributing to the circumstance of prolonged singleness for my generation.

I began to consider the progression of society's trends, the context into which my generation was born, analyzing them through the filter of my faith.

In the meantime, I took comfort in the fact that at least one nice-looking, Christian man thought I seemed a normal and nice enough female to engage in conversation. Perhaps the jury is still out, but maybe that doesn't make me an old maid just yet.

NOTES

1. Betsy Israel, *Bachelor Girl: The Secret History of Single Women in the Twentieth Century* (New York: HarperCollins, 2002), 16.
2. "U.S. Census Bureau Reports Men and Women Wait Longer to Get Married," U.S. Census Bureau, November 10, 2010, http://census.gov/newsroom/releases/archives/families_households/cb10-174.html.
3. A.J. Keisling, *Where Have All the Good Men Gone?: Why So Many Christian Women are Remaining Single* (Eugene, OR: Harvest House Publishers, 2008), 35.
4. "Generation X," Wikipedia, http://en.wikipedia.org/wiki/Generation_X.
5. Timothy Keller, *Counterfeit Gods: The Empty Promises of Money, Sex, and Power, and the Only Hope That Matters* (New York: Dutton, 2009), 39.
6. Debbie Maken, "Rethinking the Gift of Singleness," *Boundless*, January 19, 2006, http://www.boundless.org/2005/articles/a0001199.cfm.
7. Lori Smith, *The Single Truth: Challenging the Misconceptions of Singleness with God's Consuming Truth* (Shippensburg, PA: Treasury House, 2002), 66.
8. Timothy Keller, "Sexuality and Christian Hope," April 18, 2004, MP3 audio file, http://sermons2.redeemer.com/sermons/sexuality-and-christian-hope.

"Why is finding true love these days like searching for the Holy Grail?"

- Maureen Jenkins[I]

– Chapter 2 –
Victim or Conqueror?

The woman on the other end of the phone sounded desperate, like her closet doors were about to burst. She admitted she cried a lot with disappointment over her single status.

"I still had some hope before hitting my forties," she says. But now, at forty-two, living in a new city where she moved to work with a ministry, she knows few people her age, let alone single Christian men. She prays regularly for marriage and motherhood. And her mother prays that for her, too, because she longs for grandchildren.

"I feel the pressure to fulfill my mother's expectations and dreams. I feel loss for her as well. Not only have I been let down, but God is letting my mom down. I feel like that's a large struggle for me," she says. Yet, she acknowledges God's goodness and faithfulness in her life.

God is letting us down.

I listened to this dear woman without feelings of judgment. I understand her pain. As believers, we trust in a God who has plans for our lives, a God who created us for marriage. Couldn't He bring a husband with just a word if He wanted to? He is a God of miracles. And how many times have I felt that getting married would require one?

Is God behind our generation's circumstance of prolonged singleness?

JUNE CLEAVER GONE MISSING

It turns out that *Where Have All the Good Men Gone?* author A. J. Keisling wondered the same thing. She says she "has to believe [God] is working behind the scenes to draw two hearts together at just the right time," but the "pragmatic" side of her is interested in the reasons why our generation is so different from previous ones.[2]

God is working, but so is something else. We're not living in "Leave it to Beaver" days anymore.

My mom watched that iconic program on television when she was in high school. At the time she was dating my dad, whom she thought resembled Beaver's handsome older brother, Wally Cleaver. (And he actually did!) For her, the show projected realistic expectations when it came to being a future Mrs. Cleaver: marriage after high school, having children, and wearing pearls as she vacuumed the house before her husband came home (okay, maybe not the part about the pearls).

Today, a season of singleness is the norm after high school and college. But for many of us, that season stretches ever onward, until extended singleness has become a trend. We live in the "Sex in the City" era, with women portrayed as single, promiscuous professionals, unsure whether they will ever find "true love." The Wally Cleavers seem to be few and far between.

As Keisling says, our world's culture works against us. It swarms around us like dirty flood waters as we try to paddle upstream. Are we really "lost girls" who got caught in the current with the debris of a sinful society? Keisling quotes Maken:

> In the church, instead of acknowledging that singles are operating in the most dysfunctional mating scheme known to world history, we simply presume on the Lord and his sovereignty to override our collective recklessness. Instead of recognizing that many single women are victims because of the deficits in the present construct, we dismiss their unwanted status as simply "God's will."

I'll say "amen" to Maken's point in her original article: "Our contemporary belief that Scripture validates singleness *en masse* is a modern invention that has sprouted only in this generation."[3] In other words, God's will for our generation is not prolonged singleness.

But something she said doesn't set well with me: that I'm merely a victim. A victim of the world and of my circumstances.

I get that sentiment, though. I'm tempted to think and live with a victim's mindset sometimes. When I look at the circumstances, both inside and outside the Church, it is easy to feel like I've slid, unnoticed, into the black X of a forgotten generation. Like one of the many unlucky ones who may not get picked before my expiration date.

But that's not the way I want to live my life, and not the way, I think, God sees my circumstances. "Yet amid all these things," Paul wrote, "we are more than conquerors and gain a surpassing victory through Him Who loved us" (Romans 8:37, AMP). If this is the truth, and it is, then I need to understand what it means to live as a conqueror when it's so easy to feel like a victim.

Perhaps one place to begin is by examining society's trends, the circumstances that threaten. Maybe I need to ask this question: Have I bought into the world's philosophy?

THE WOMAN WHO DOES EVERYTHING

She wears a shimmering strapless gown, her waist tiny, collarbones outlined by smooth and impeccable skin. Her hair waves away from her face, a small wheat field in the wind. And she's on the cover of the May 2008 issue of *Vogue*.

"How does Gwyneth Paltrow—movie star…rock wife, and supermom—make it all look so easy?" the story's headline reads. Trying to be a stay-at-home mom who, at the time, also worked as a high-profile actress, maintained a contract with a beauty product company, participated in a cooking show and managed a household shared with a famous musician husband, Paltrow said, "I think the thing that drives most working mothers crazy is this idea that they can't do everything: 'I don't know what to wear. I don't know what to cook. I can't work and do this and that and the other.' But I find that as long as you're not depressed, if you simplify everything, you can do anything."[4]

One of my forty-something single friends says this: "The woman who does everything is looked on as heroic, a role model for the rest of us."

And, I will add: In this day and age, not only can women do it all, we *should* do it all. And we should do it all *well*—albeit simplified. Whether single or married, that's what women's equality with men has come to mean. We can do what the women of past generations did as housewives and mothers, vacuuming our houses but saving the pearls for later as we pursue what the modern man does in business, politics, or society. Never mind that it might lead to depression.

The woman who does everything—that's the culture we grew up in, the one that June Cleaver knew nothing about, the one that spawned a singleness trend.

It's not that motherhood and careers are incompatible, or that life should return to the way it was in the "olden days." The Feminist Movement, which effected many of our societal changes, helped women's social experience begin to align with the reality that God created them equal to men. But for all the good that movement was meant to bring—good perhaps even orchestrated by God Himself—a worldly spirit behind it has grown steadily, stealthily over time. The pendulum has swung far to the other side. The pearl of Woman is losing its luster. Let me explain what I mean.

The pressure of "everything" is part of what delays marriage—trend reports often cite the female pursuit of education and careers as causes. As singleness continues to extend and our generation ages, one emerging trend signals that singleness need not exclude motherhood from the "everything" list.

Enter "The Single Mom Through Choice" concept. One article on this subject states, "Although divorce is still the most common way in which women become single mothers, more than forty percent of today's single moms have never been married, suggesting a significant shift in societal attitudes."[5]

Another article supports this statement with statistical information from 2008. "Birthrates have risen for all women ages thirty and older… The rate increases have been sharpest for women in the oldest age groups—forty-seven percent for women ages thirty-five to thirty-nine and eighty percent for women ages forty to forty-four, for example." After further assessing the data, the writer concludes, "All this seems to indicate that more older, single women are choosing to have babies on their own—for 'the joy' of having them—after realizing or deciding they're not going to get married."[6]

Here's the point: Heroic women can do everything, *without the men*. That spirit behind feminism, that doing-of-everything, is the undertow of one single mother's experience. Feminist writer Lori Gottleib selected the father of her child from a donor sperm bank. One day she and another single mom by choice took their children to the park, noting that they had finally realized their dream of motherhood. She describes the experience in an article.

> But it was also decidedly not the dream. The dream, like that of our mothers and their mothers from time immemorial, was to fall in love, get married, and live happily ever after. Of course, we'd be loath to admit it in this day and age, but ask any soul-baring forty-year-old single heterosexual woman what she most longs for in life, and she probably won't tell you it's a better career or a smaller waistline or a bigger apartment. Most likely, she'll say that what she really wants is a husband (and, by extension, a child).
>
> To the outside world, of course, we still call ourselves feminists and insist—vehemently, even—that we're independent and self-sufficient and don't believe in any of that damsel-in-distress stuff,

> but in reality, we aren't fish who can do without a bicycle, we're women who want a traditional family. And despite growing up in an era when the centuries-old mantra to get married young was finally (and, it seemed, refreshingly) replaced by encouragement to postpone that milestone in pursuit of high ideals (education! career! but also true love!), every woman I know—no matter how successful and ambitious, how financially and emotionally secure—feels panic, occasionally coupled with desperation, if she hits thirty and finds herself unmarried.[7]

Gottleib's point in this article is that while finding true love is desirable and ideal, it's not likely to happen. She concludes that it is better to settle for someone because marrying a good-enough man creates the necessary "infrastructure" to have a family. "Based on my observations, in fact, settling will probably make you happier in the long run, since many of those who marry with great expectations become more disillusioned with each passing year," she says.[8]

Gottleib, however, only reaches this conclusion *after* she's given birth to her child, alone. In a prior article about her pregnancy, she appears unwilling to "settle," saying, "Whereas women of a certain age used to marry their boyfriends in order to have children, nowadays it no longer sounds counterintuitive to hear a single woman say that she, like me, *broke up with her* boyfriend in order to have a baby."[9]

In other words, today's older single woman should either settle for a less-than-desirable man or just go without one altogether. And either way, she is capable of doing anything.

Never mind the deep desires of her heart, nor the ways of God.

THAT SPECK OF DUST

She had everything any woman could ever want or need. She had the perfect husband; and their love was joyous, beautiful, pure, nothing held back. They lived together in a fragrant, flowering garden where it never rained. She even took walks in the evenings with God Himself.

Her name was Eve. And if ever there was a woman who got to experience the fullness and freedom of God's plan for femininity, it would have been her. In spite of all this, that spirit hidden inside the Feminist Movement was planted first in Eve's soul through the lilting whisper of a serpent: self-sufficiency.

The woman who can do anything and everything. *Without God.* That one thing the Lord had said was off limits—eating that fruit from the Tree of Knowledge of Good and Evil? It would make her like God. The serpent's suggestion raised questions about whether there was more for Eve to experience than she already had, something better. Was there, perhaps, more for her to be than the woman she was?

This is when that seed of self-sufficiency first took root. She tasted the forbidden fruit. Savored it, catching with her tongue the sweetness that dripped down her lips. She ran to her husband, and he tasted it, too—who knows, maybe reluctantly—but he did it all the same. And from that point forward, the original God-ordained partnership of marriage fell under the consequences of sin.

Besides pain in childbirth, Woman's consequence would be desire for her husband, who would rule over her (Genesis 3:16). While it isn't completely clear what the original Hebrew phrase, "desire for your husband," means, "the expression carries the idea that, remembering their joint-rule in the Garden, she would desire to dominate her husband."[10] Eve would now desire to have as her own the place of authority she had disdained.

To be one's own authority, the deception that something or someone besides God—including relationship with a man—can bring greater, ultimate fulfillment: this is now part of every woman's fleshly inheritance from Eve. If we become our own authority, we will do whatever we think is necessary to get what we desire. It is, perhaps, the speck of dust, the thorn, that the pearl of unredeemed womanhood grows around.

It is no surprise, then, that the germ of self-sufficiency has blossomed into a movement that goes beyond the social equality of women to the total independence and even dominance of women. The woman who does everything is really saying, "I can do everything myself, and I certainly don't need a man to help me." And men's role as protector and pursuer is reduced to what Gottleib describes as "that damsel-in-distress stuff."

Sure, women today want true love and the commitment and security marriage is supposed to bring. But we are told we need not be dependent on husbands, men, or anyone. We can make our own money, become successful through hard work, and choose our own goals regardless of family needs. We have the right to put ourselves first.

But truthfully, you just can't have it both ways. We were all born into this battle—humanity against God, Satan against humanity, flesh against Spirit. And for this reason, that spirit of the world has affected us in the Church, whether we realize it or not.

My friend is in her mid-forties. She works all day at a high-profile company in the financial world, a "man's world," she says. The married woman at the next desk talks to her husband on the phone, and it sounds like she is speaking to a child.

My friend is mortified. It's just like the reality shows and sitcoms that feature husbands and wives, she says. The husband is portrayed as an idiot who makes mistakes, while the wife is self-assured and in control. The husband left his wife, but she treated him like trash. *Men are stupid, and women are the only smart ones.*

"Even the women at work tell me I'm the smart one because I'm single," she says. "I can do whatever I want and don't have kids or a husband to chase after to get him to do what he has to be doing... There's a lot of controlling women around."

That old-self within us, that dead and going-nowhere life, perks up at the trail of worldly logic. Our souls take in the messages and images—the entertainment that portrays men as passive, weak, unable to lead, and even acceptably effeminate. The wives who call the shots and disdain their husbands. The women who chase after men, and the men who coast through life passively on the tracks of an extended adolescence.

If we're not vigilant in all things, measuring them against the Word of God, we begin to wonder what's supposed to be normal.

SPEAKING OF WHAT'S SUPPOSED TO BE NORMAL

Once, I found myself sitting next to a Baby Boomer and his daughter at a conference dinner. He asked what I was writing about, and we talked about why there are so many older single women in the world. He noted another trend—that men in their twenties don't seem to be ready for marriage or interested in finding a wife because they're "too busy playing video games." Men, he said, seem to be taking longer to grow up. And he's right. Stephanie Coontz, author and teacher on the subject of marriage and family, writes this:

> In the 1950s, when half of all American women were already married in their teens, marriage was an almost mandatory first step toward adulthood. It was considered the best way to make a man grow up, and in an economy where steady jobs and rising real wages were widely available, that often worked… Today, however, there are plenty of other ways to grow up... Marriage has become another step, perhaps even the final rather than the first step, in the transition to adulthood…"[11]

Take the 2006 movie *Failure to Launch*, which I could not bring myself to see. It's the story of a thirty-five-year-old man still living at home with his parents. The parents hire a single woman to lure their son into mature adulthood using her femininity as a deceptive tool. One reviewer of the movie says this:

> At least according to trend articles, more and more young people are living with their parents well into their twenties and even into their thirties. So the idea behind Tom Dey's "Failure to Launch," if only mildly clever, is reasonably realistic. Sarah Jessica Parker's Paula is a life coach of sorts who hires herself out to not-so-empty nesters, using her alleged charm and wit to inspire self-confidence and self-sufficiency in their sons so they'll finally have the will, and the desire, to leave home.[12]

This is not a comedy; it is a tragedy. And many people think it's normal.

It is part of the enemy's strategy to destroy what God started in that generous Garden: marriage, family, and the abundance of inter-dependent relationships built on love. Our society's trends are the fruit of his work that started long ago.

AN OFFERING OF POP BEADS

"Single women have a dreadful propensity for being poor. Which is one very strong argument in favor of matrimony," Jane Austen wrote in the nineteenth century.[13]

In her day, and later in America in the early twentieth century, women sought to escape marriage because they longed for something other than to be restricted by their husbands and fathers socially, intellectually, and professionally. Women didn't want to be property in their households, and for many, singleness was the only alternative.

In these women early feminism is recognized because they deliberately avoided marriage. And for many years, feminism and singleness have held hands, despite the fact that one of feminism's goals when it began in the eighteenth century was to grant a certain class of women the right to vote.

Fast forward to a major shift. From the 1960s through the 1980s—the birth dates of Generation X—what is known as the Second Wave of Feminism focused on the personal lives of women and inequality in a male-dominated culture. It targeted stay-at-home wives and mothers who longed for more than what June Cleaver or the more progressive TV character Carol Brady experienced. The focus moved from women's social and political rights to their "personal rights" of marriage and motherhood.[14]

As we grew up, women moved from behind the apron to behind the workstation. They traded the house dress for the business suit. By the time we were old enough to enter the workforce, many women had also traded caring for children all day at home for finding the right day-care center for their children so they could go to work.

The shifting perspective of motherhood went far deeper than the option to not stay home to raise kids. In the most twisted of extremes, feminism endorsed the so-called right of a pregnant woman to decide whether she even wants to give birth to the child in her womb. Abortion became legal in 1973, right in the middle of the Generation X birth dates. Between 1973 and 1984, the ratio of abortions to live births increased and peaked in the United States. Since 1984, that ratio has steadily declined, making Generation X the most aborted generation thus far.[15]

My point, ladies, is that we were born into the thick of a very fierce battle. I'm glad single women don't have to be poor today. But do we have to take on the whole world, by ourselves? When it comes to marriage and motherhood, the stakes are higher in our generation than ever before. The string of pearls that society has offered us as women are really pop beads. Deep down, men don't really want to fight for a string of plastic beads. They want the real thing. The question is, do we really know what that is?

Thank God, Jesus has already won the war for us through the cross. In Him, Man and Woman stand redeemed, their true identities waiting to be claimed. Whether we become victims of the battle is up to us.

RECLAIMING THE REAL THING

She was steering her ten-year-old Chevette down the highway after a weekend visit with her parents. She was in her thirties and single. It had been a lonely season. God seemed distant, and His provision slow in coming. *Why am I still alone?*

Suddenly, her car went dead. Annette pulled to the side of the isolated road, and popped the hood. *What do I know about cars?* She didn't even have a cell phone.

Oh Lord, please protect me. Send someone to help me.

Within minutes a man stopped on the opposite side of the road and began to walk her way, but something about him made her afraid. He stood at the engine and looked it over. And over. *Why is it taking so long?*

He tinkered. Five minutes. Ten minutes. A motorcycle rumbled by, then stopped. A leather-clad man got off the bike and walked back toward Annette and the stranger. An impulsive fear-clad thought: *They are in this together.*

But the biker went to the engine, and within minutes, the other man suddenly left. Without a word. By this time, the biker's girlfriend had arrived, and they determined the car needed a power jump. As the biker turned around to get his motorcycle, Annette saw big letters on the back of his leather jacket: *Bikers for Jesus.*

Tears filled her eyes. The car surged to life. The biker closed the hood, and Annette called out, "Thank you!" Before she could drive away, the man came around to her window. He looked directly into her eyes and spoke without hesitation: "God always provides."

And then he was gone.

Damsel in distress? That day, Annette certainly was. And I know, in many smaller and sometimes bigger ways, I have been. You have been.

Does that make us victims? Should we become the woman who does everything, without help, without a man?

I know I can't be that woman. I can't hang a towel rod and get it to stay in the wall to save my life. I can't change the oil in my car (nor, I confess, do I want to). I can't take care of a house, car, yard, and job with no help from anyone.

Sometimes, as long-time single women, it feels like we have no choice but to be self-sufficient. Don't we have to take control because we don't have a partner to provide help and support? Don't we have to figure out the solutions for broken cars or burst pipes, pay the bills and clean the house, fitting it all in between the overgrown hedges and the unbalanced checkbook? We are adults, responsible for stewarding all God has given us. As one of my forty-something friends pointed out, it's not appropriate for us to live with our parents because we aren't married—not at our age!

But we do have a choice. We can live in self-sufficiency as the woman who does everything, "Christianizing" it by adding church and ministry involvement to the list. Or we can live as a woman dependent on and submitted to God.

The truth is, we are not alone. *God always provides.*

In those moments when help feels far away, I do what Annette did. I pray: *God, please send someone to help me.* Many times I have stood on Psalm 46:1 (NAS), "God is our refuge and strength, a very present help in trouble." And every time He has answered. He gives me an idea of what to do or who to call, or He sends someone to help without my having to ask.

There are days, overwhelming days, when job and house and events and responsibilities make me breathless, and I arrive home to find that someone has mowed the yard for me. There was that yucky wake-up-to-a-swarm-of-flying-ants day. There are broken air conditioner days and clogged kitchen sink days and what's-that-noise-my-car-is-making days. And my Very Present Help is always there.

All we have to do is ask. And sometimes it means reaching out to ask others—*even men*—for help. Like the time my lawn mower bellowed smoke, and I asked my kind neighbor to assess the damage. Sometimes it's simply humbling ourselves as God moves others to serve without our asking. Like the time another neighbor showed up with a chain saw as I stood in my front yard wondering how I was going to remove my fallen pear tree from the street.

Believe it or not, the "Proverbs 31 woman" models this for us. But wait—doesn't she look like the woman who does everything? And doesn't she have a partner to help her? What's the difference between her and the heroic supermom on the cover of *Vogue*?

She's not depressed with the striving. No, this woman smiles at the future (Proverbs 31:25), because she knows she can handle it. Not by herself. Not because she has a husband.

There's another reason, called out by one woman writing about the Proverbs 31 woman.

> She is highlighted right in the center of the Bible... Before you know what her life is like, you see into her heart: "The heart of her husband safely trusts in her; she will do him good and not evil all the days of her life." ...Where is submission? It shows in her dedicated heart and priorities and vision. Every one in her household is well cared for . . . and she herself? "Her clothing is silk and purple." ...Submission is a life dedicated to God, your husband, your household and your own wide ranging possibility! What does the "keeper at home" do (Titus 2:5)? What does her life look like? Here is your model. Your life can be an exciting adventure as hers. Looking inside for how you are "wired" and to God for wisdom, you will succeed.[16]

True womanhood is reclaimed through submission to God, a natural part of Eve's spirit before she met the snake. A woman who fears the Lord—*she* shall be praised (verse 30). This is the woman whose worth is far above rubies (verse 10). This is the gleaming pearl that excels in all aspects of her femininity (verse 29).

Whether you are a keeper of home, seller to merchants, or a sower of silk; whether married or maiden, submission to the Father-King is your secret, is mine. He is our sufficiency. In Him we are more than conquerors—of worldly ideas and ideals.

Feminine identity and prosperity, reputation and success, come not from the pursuit of personal rights or selfish ambition. It all comes from serving and helping others as one already helped, as one submitted to receiving what God wants to give. As one who is more than a conqueror through the love of Christ, a love that provides everything we need.

Say the experts, "Pearls are very soft and need special care."[17] The same describes the pearl of Woman, designed to complement the platinum of Man. The Bridegroom-Husbandman knows exactly how to provide special care for His daughters. And He knows that pearls are meant to be worn,[18] exhibited, and enjoyed; valued for their beauty and their function.

That's what I'm after. That's why I can't live as a victim, in my thinking or in my experiences. And thank God, because He is sovereign over even worldly circumstances, I don't have to.

NOTES

1. Maureen Jenkins, "Boldly going -- alone?: Chicago Gen X women talk about why it's so," *Chicago Sun Times*, April 5, 2006, page 50.
2. AJ Keisling, *Where Have All the Good Men Gone?: Why So Many Christian Women are Remaining Single* (Eugene, OR: Harvest House Publishers, 2008), 38.
3. Debbie Maken, "Rethinking the Gift of Singleness," *Boundless*, January 19, 2006, http://www.boundless.org/2005/articles/a0001199.cfm.
4. Plum Sykes, "Gwyneth's Guide to Life," *Vogue*, May 2008, http://vogue.com/magazine/article/gwyneth-paltrow-gwyneths-guide-to-life/.
5. Neilia Sherman, "On Your Own: Becoming a Single Mom Through Choice," *MomsToday.com,* accessed April 27, 2011, http://momstoday.com/articles/single-mother/single-mom-by-choice-2787/ (site discontinued).
6. Maura Kelly, "More Women Choosing to Have Babies Solo: A Good Thing?" www.marieclaire.com, May 7, 2010 (article no longer available).
7. Lori Gottleib, "Marry Him! The Case for Settling for Mr. Good Enough," *Atlantic Magazine*, March 2008, http://theatlantic.com/magazine/archive/2008/03/marry-him/6651/.
8. Ibid.

9. Lori Gottlieb, "The XY Files," *Atlantic Magazine*, September 2005, http:// www.theatlantic.com/magazine/archive/2005/09/the-xy-files/4172/.

10. R. Russell Bixler, B.A., M.A., M.Div, Note on Genesis 3:16 in the *Spirit-Filled Life Bible*, ed. Jack W. Hayford, Litt.D. (Nashville: Thomas Nelson, 1991), 9.

11. Stephanie Coontz, "Is Marriage Becoming Obsolete?" CNN, November 22, 2010, http://cnn.com/2010/OPINION.

12. Stephanie Zacharek, review of *Failure to Launch*, Paramount Pictures, Salon.com, March 10, 2006, http://salon.com/2006/03/10/failure_2/.

13. "Jane Austen: Biography," Shmoop.com, November 11, 2008, http://shmoop.com/jane-austen/ biography.html.

14. "Feminist Movement," *Wikipedia*, last modified December 29, 2011, http://en.wikipedia.org/wiki/Feminist_movement.

15. "Annual Abortion Statistics," Abort73.com, last updated November 15, 2011, http://abort73.com/abortion_facts/us_abortion_ statistics/.

16. Elizabeth Julin, "Re-Understanding Submission . . . a Role Model," *Submission is Not Silence* (blog), April 28, 2011, http://submissionisnotsilence.com/2011/04/re-understanding-submission-a-role-model/.

17. "How to Care for Your Cultured Pearls," Pearl Oasis, http://www.pearloasis.com/care.html.

18. "Why Do Pearls Turn Yellow?" *Jewelry Secrets,* http://www.jewelry-secrets.com/Gemstones/Pearl/Pearls-Turn-Yellow/Why-Do-Pearl-Necklaces-Turn-Yellow-Color.html.

"God did not let His Sovereignty slip from His fingers."

- Betsie ten Boom

– Chapter 3 –

CHOICE *or* SOVEREIGNTY?

The question floated over the heads of Bible college students like an autumn leaf on a windless day, no hint of a coming storm.

Do you believe that God has only one person out there for you?

The class was Marriage and Family. I was one of the students. The question slowly sank in, then the energetic discussion began.

I was about twenty years old. *Yes*, I thought. Only *one* person in the world could ever qualify as my soul mate, my one true love, the man of my dreams. It was a matter of *destiny*. Indisputable fact, in my romance novel, fairytale-influenced mind. But within minutes, I was forced to reconsider.

As students began to voice their opinions, difficult questions arose for me. *What about people who remarried after a spouse died or left? Who was the true soul mate, the true love destined for the person who married more than once?*

Twenty years later, details lost, I can only recall how the discussion ended. The professor's response to the last comment was, "Then that would mean you can marry the wrong person, wouldn't it?"

Yes, from my internal monologue. *You can miss your destiny.* I was worried that I might.

That's as far as my thinking went that day, but it helped to begin in me a years-long intellectual tiff between God's sovereignty and humanity's free choice. How "fixed" was God's will, really? How much could our choices alter it?

Twenty years ago, I thought my destiny was set in stone. But I've been forced to reconsider.

OF SOVEREIGNTY AND DESTINY

I am in my mid-twenties, a working woman now, still clinging to fairytales and happily-ever-after. Still thinking I can predict how God is going to fulfill my marital destiny, unaware of the risk in my mindset.

A Christian colleague admits he hadn't been sure whether his wife was the one God had intended for him to marry. However, he believes that as they sought God and worked on their marriage, she became the person that God had for him. She became "God's will."

The tug-of-war between sovereignty and free choice stirs again. I understand that remaining faithful to your marriage, whether you chose the right person or not, is God's will. But how could a person who wasn't God's choice for you turn into His choice at some point? What happened to the person God had originally picked out for you? Was that person's destiny ruined? Would God change His mind about such things? I eventually let the conflict settle down again somewhere in a corner of my spirit.

Years later, I wonder what that man says now about God's will. He and his wife are divorced, and he is married to someone else. Meanwhile, I am still single. At forty. Wondering if it's possible that I missed my destiny after all. Or maybe I've simply misunderstood it, the idea of a fixed destiny, of God's sovereignty.

Over the years, I've thought about God's sovereignty when I consider the amazing ways He's worked in my life—how, in His sovereignty, He allowed me to be born into a Christian family. With His sovereign hand, He protected me from harm in so many ways. He led me to a church that would teach me how to walk in an intimate relationship with Him. *Sovereignty.* It's a good word.

But God's sovereignty doesn't seem like a good thing when I consider the unexpected turns of life—how, in His sovereignty, He allowed my niece to be born with a malfunctioning heart. With His sovereign hand, He let me stay single through two decades of physical youth. He allowed, in His sovereignty, my dear mother to die of the cancer we believed He was going to heal. *Sovereignty.* It's a confusing word.

It's a word that carries weight, like its meaning: *rule, supremacy, dominance.* Applied to God, it couldn't be more authoritative. He has the ultimate say, the final word. He reigns, influences, orchestrates, directs, decides.

It seems a simple enough concept. Throw in the fact that God created people with free choice, and it gets more complex. Especially when those choice-making people have surrendered themselves to the one sovereign God. Circumstance is the thing caught in the middle, the rope between two truths that don't seem to touch, truths that pull back and forth, back and forth, with the weight of changing circumstances. Circumstances influenced by many choices, heavy enough to make us feel like victims, serious enough to make us wonder about God's authoritative rule over them.

Which leads me to the most important thing in all of it: Relationship with God. Trusting Him with my heart, which balances on the rope between choice and sovereignty. Walking rightly with Him—not resigned, fatalistic, victimized—but walking, rather, with the vibrancy and energy of His Spirit within me, as more than a conqueror.

How do I do that? Do I accept long-term singleness, which seems like less than what He intended for me as a woman? Do I assume a prayerful desire for something that seems like His will is going to make it happen?

It seems impossible and risky, this task of reconciling God's design for marriage with my circumstance of prolonged singleness. Of understanding God's sovereignty in circumstances that oppose His design. Of trusting His sovereignty while wondering if it has prevented me from experiencing the fulfillment of a desire He placed within me.

HOW GOD WORKS

Circumstances were bad. Sin and immorality corrupted her country. Their long-time archenemy dominated them. And still she couldn't get pregnant.

She was one of God's people, an Israelite. Surely it wasn't God's will for them to be overrun by the Philistines. Yet, the majority of people had chosen to walk contrary to God. Long ago, He clearly spelled out the rules for living in the Promised Land. Collective disobedience had reaped its harvest.

But she and her husband feared God. She hated, perhaps, what was going on in the nation. She mourned, perhaps, what wasn't going on in her own life.

Until the day the Man appeared. Ordinary, maybe, at first a regular stranger. But then—that shining face, sunlight-white with beautiful features showing through, hard to describe later to her husband. But she had to try, oh, she had to try. Because he looked like he came from heaven. And he told her they would have a son.

When that promised son was born, they named him Samson.

As I read this story in Judges 13 one morning, the sovereignty versus circumstance struggle weighed again on my mind. This couple, Manoah and his wife, lived in a society that didn't fear God. That feels familiar.

How much of that worldly philosophy influenced their lives, their thoughts? What was the strength of their faith? Was their barrenness a part of God's overall judgment on their nation?

Nothing in Scripture suggests childlessness was a particular punishment for them when other couples in the world were still having children. And nothing in Scripture explicitly explains why they, specifically, were chosen to bear a specially-destined child out of their barrenness. But God trusted them with the responsibility of raising a man who He wanted to name judge of Israel. Was there no current adult qualified to judge? No current child being raised with the fear of God necessary for such a task?

Apparently not. God must have chosen them because they were faithful to Him even when the rest of society wasn't. They hadn't bought into the lies around them, even though their circumstances didn't seem to line up with God's design. I saw something about

God's sovereignty in their story that encouraged me. He works in the lives of people who walk with Him in faith, no matter how godless their society or disappointing their personal circumstances.

Society and disappointment and loss had not disqualified Manoah and his wife from experiencing God's work in their individual lives. They weren't left without a future and a hope because life around them went sideways or even facedown, because God's design for man and wife to have children remained unfulfilled.

Rather, God found them qualified for a special assignment that would require a miracle. In the process, He turned their disappointment over an unmet desire into the fulfillment of a dream.

And that's an example of sovereignty at work. God's decision and influence overruling circumstance, making the people involved conquerors rather than victims. Taking the circumstance and turning it into something meaningful and significant and purposeful.

I can trust in that kind of sovereignty. Then I read that when Samson grew up, something went wrong.

WHAT'S REALLY FIXED

Get her for me as a wife.

Manoah couldn't believe his ears. His wife thought her heart might stop. Samson's words choked them. His *her* referred to a Philistine girl, a daughter of the enemy, of the oppressors. Of people they really just couldn't stand, people that had no place becoming part of their family or their grandchildren's lineage.

And besides, hadn't they raised him better than this? The shining Man had said to Samson's mother, "No razor shall come upon his head, for the boy shall be a Nazirite to God from the womb, and he shall begin to deliver Israel from the hands of the Philistines" (Judges 13:5, NAS).

Manoah had wanted to meet this Man, to hear the prophecy, to be in on the instructions. He prayed for a chance to meet the Man himself, and God answered. Manoah got to hear firsthand that his son was called to be a Nazirite, someone, Numbers 6 explains, specially set apart to God, abstaining from drinking wine, cutting his hair or defiling himself by touching a dead body.

And so Samson's parents were diligent to raise him well. Their name for their son perhaps reflects their respect for the heavenly messenger and his message, for Samson means "like the sun."[1]

Perhaps Manoah recalled teaching Samson God's directive, handed down from Moses, reiterated by Joshua:

> When the Lord your God brings you into the land which you go to possess, and has cast out many nations before you…you shall make no covenant with them nor show mercy to them. Nor shall you make marriages with them. You shall not give your daughter to their son, nor take their daughter for your son. For they will turn your sons away from following Me, to serve other gods… (Deuteronomy 7:1-4, NKJV)

And now, Samson's confession of a secret Philistine infatuation.

"Is there no woman among the daughters of your relatives, or among all our people," his parents ask, "that you go to take a wife from the uncircumcised Philistines?" (Judges 14:3, NAS).

Marrying a Philistine woman should have felt like the farthest thing from God's plan for a Nazirite called to be a deliverer. And yet, this: *Get her for me, for she pleases me well!*

And that's exactly what his parents do.

But something else was at work. Something they didn't know but God chose to reveal to us in Judges 14:4. I stopped short when I read it: "But his father and mother did not know that it was of the Lord—that He was seeking an occasion to move against the Philistines" (NKJV).

It was *of the Lord?* How could Samson's choice—his free choice—of a marriage partner be *of the Lord* when it contradicted His Law? Surely she wasn't "the one" God had created especially for him. She couldn't have been his destiny.

Some commentators have written that the Lord put the idea in Samson's heart, indicating that Samson knew it would lead to an opportunity to interact with and destroy the Philistines. Wouldn't God have given him a more lawful idea for interacting with the Philistines?

Samson's phrase "she pleases me well" leads to a different conclusion. The notes in my Bible state it "literally means 'for she is right in my eyes.' It is similar to the Hebrew expression...that is translated, 'Everyone did what was right in his own eyes.'"[2] The book of Judges uses the phrase repeatedly to convey the idea that God's people were not united in following Him. They constantly strayed, reaping oppression by their enemies until God sent a judge.

It's a phrase that meant they were making choices—and creating circumstances—contrary to God's will.

It seems even though Samson was a Nazirite, society's philosophy, society's "normal," had made its way into his heart. He was affected by the spiritual climate of his nation and, like everyone else, made a choice based on his own desires, not on God's.

Nevertheless, God had plans to use that choice to accomplish His purpose of bringing deliverance from the Philistines. The notes in my Bible put it this way: "God did not approve of Samson's decision to break the law, but He used the circumstances for His purposes and for His glory."[3]

As I thought about this note, the theological tug-of-war within me quieted a little. Sovereignty doesn't mean everything that happens is God's will. It doesn't imply fixed *circumstances*. It implies fixed *purpose*.

It means that in spite of and in the midst of—*and maybe even because of*—everything that happens, God accomplishes His purpose. And His purpose ultimately is His will. The idea bends the mind a bit.

God used Samson's wrong choice, which created a circumstance outside of God's will, to work out His purpose—His destiny—for Samson's life. Samson's parents went with him to meet the Philistine woman, and marriage plans were made. When the big week arrived, Samson's bride spoiled his wedding riddle. Samson had promised thirty garments and changes of clothing if his Philistine friends couldn't guess the answer to his riddle. They couldn't, and they pressured his bride into telling them. To make good on the clothing he owed in losing the bet, Samson killed thirty Philistine men.

God used the wedding conflict to begin a liberating work for His people through Samson. Further interaction with his Philistine wife, which tragically resulted in her cruel murder, led Samson to other acts of vengeance against the Philistines.

I can't help but wonder if God had a different wife picked out for Samson—or, depending on your view of marital destiny, an appropriate selection of women for Samson to choose from. Could it not have been God's will that he enjoy life with a God-fearing Israelite woman, raising the next generation in His ways? Couldn't God have used other events to accomplish Samson's work of deliverance?

He could have. But He used the circumstances created by the choices that all the characters in this story made. Through those circumstances—whether they aligned with His will or not—God fulfilled His own purpose. A. W. Tozer says, as sovereign, God is "free to do whatever He wills to do anywhere at any time to carry out His eternal purpose in every single detail without interference."[4]

Despite his wrong choices, Samson lived a Nazirite life, set apart to serve God. But when he gave away the secret to his strength, causing his enemies to cut his hair and break his Nazirite vow, he experienced circumstances opposite of His God-given destiny. The Philistines put him in prison, but Samson's hair grew long again. God allowed him one more opportunity to fulfill his purpose.

Samson leaned with his arms against the pillars of the pagan temple. He felt that old, once-familiar strength rush through his chest, ripple through his biceps. He began to push, and as he did, he asked that God would let him die with this last act of vengeance on his enemies.

The temple crashed upon hundreds of Philistines, and God granted Samson his final request. I can't help but wonder if he died with regret about some of his life choices.

I think so.

HELD IN HIS HAND

She lay sick on the only cot in a filthy prison cell built for one person. It confined four or five.

It was spring 1944. Betsie ten Boom, her sister Corrie, their father and many other friends and family members had been arrested by German police in February. There had been an early morning buzz at the door, an unexpected rush of officers into their home. The Jews hiding in their old Dutch house dashed through Corrie's closet into the secret room. They were never discovered, but their benefactors suffered.

A few days after the arrest, Betsie's elderly and godly father caught pneumonia at the savage prison. He died alone on a cot in an impersonal hallway. Betsie had loved, respected, and lived with him her entire life. She had supported him, served with him, risked danger with him. She received the heartbreaking news of his death later that spring, through a letter.

She looked to God's sovereignty to find His purpose. "So our dear father has now been promoted to Glory. And how? The Lord Himself crowned his head with the martyr's crown," she wrote to her niece.[5]

> I often thought that a person in whom Christ was shown to such full advantage, who lived so close to the Saviour, to whom the eternal things were so real, and who had the gift of prayer in such a wonderful way—such a person has all the conditions for becoming a martyr… The Lord gave him a happy life, such as not one in 10,000 has. Just before his death the Lord took him away from his dear ones in order to be able to give him the crown of honor. God did not let His Sovereignty slip from His fingers. No, this all had to be this way, even my being here in prison…[6]

Even my being here in prison. In the midst of her own suffering and unjust imprisonment, Betsie looked for the purpose of God. She found it in His sovereignty, which honored her aged father with a death that identified him with the suffering and death of Christ.

She could not have known that she too would die a martyr. Although her season of cruel imprisonment and tribulation—the last season of her life—had just begun, she refused to see herself as a victim of the Germans, the harsh guards, or even of Satan. Instead, she looked to God and found hope in His purposes for her in the midst of her pain. She knew He would not let her "slip from His fingers."

In the midst of all that, there was one circumstance she didn't seem to regard much. Betsie ten Boom was never married.

If Betsie could face the enemy's worst work in her generation with a pure and hopeful heart, I can too. My circumstances may not be the same as hers, but the enemy is the same. Through every age, when it comes to the lives of His faithful people, God is not about to let His sovereignty slip from His fingers. We may feel powerless to change our circumstances, our society, or our world. But we are not hopeless victims who will miss out on God's goodness. Betsie certainly wouldn't say that she did.

When it comes to His children's lives, God always has the upper hand. It is His hand that has the power to transform us through our circumstances. To save a marriage that is falling apart, to bring marriage after years of singleness. To open the barren womb and close the door of sickness. To make a single woman imprisoned in a Nazi concentration camp more than a conqueror. As I read Corrie ten Boom's description of life in that camp, Betsie was clearly the hero of her story. The Spirit of God through Betsie brought peace, goodness, and transformation wherever she went.

As people of God, it is up to us to lay hold of the truth that we are more than conquerors, first by believing it; second, by walking so close to God that it becomes our experience. Even in circumstances not meant to be.

Sometimes, though, in the midst of these circumstances, something gets in the way of our believing and laying hold. And it's something we can't ignore or stuff away. We must deal with it before we can take hold of God's sovereign purpose and anticipate redemption. It is a thing called disappointment. And no matter how deep it goes, God has made a way for us to get through to the other side.

NOTES

1. "Shimshown," *The NAS Old Testament Hebrew Lexicon,* http://www.biblestudytools.com/lexicons/hebrew/nas/shimshown.html.
2. Cheryl Lynn Hetherington, S.T.D., M.A., M.Phil., Ph.D., Note on Judges 14:3 in the *Spirit-Filled Life Bible*, ed. Jack W. Hayford, Litt.D. (Nashville: Thomas Nelson, 1991), 370.
3. Hetherington, Note on Judges 14:4 in the *Spirit-Filled Life Bible*, 370.
4. A.W. Tozer, *The Knowledge of the Holy* (New York: Walker & Company, 1996), 206.
5. Corrie ten Boom, *Prison Letters* (Old Tappan, NJ: Fleming H. Revell Company, 1975), 20.
6. Ibid., 20-21.

"Thou hast not *that*, my child,
But thou hast me;
And am not I alone enough for thee?
I know it all,
Know how thy heart was set
Upon this joy which is not given yet."

- Amy Carmichael[1]

– Chapter 4 –

Hope or Disappointment

I sit in a classroom full of writers at a conference. My fortieth birthday is only a few weeks behind me. More than ever before, I feel the pressure of *old maid* against my heart. I feel conspicuous, as if everyone can tell I just turned forty, as if *spinster* splinters my features with its epithet.

The writers introduce themselves. I can't bear to announce the subject of my writing to the group. I usually speak freely about my topic, but the sting of still-single-at-forty smarts fresh. I swallow the word *singleness* whole, much like I did boiled Brussels sprouts as a child, and, instead, only say I write nonfiction. The next person introduces herself, then the next. Suddenly, I hear a woman say that her writing is about grieving singleness over forty. Her words rush at me like cold water to the face. My mind snaps alert. I jot down her name: Sharyn Kopf (now the author of *Spinstered*).

Never before had I heard someone describe the disappointment of prolonged singleness as grief. *That's it. That's exactly how I feel.*

I know I need to shake off the lies that I'm an old maid, undeserving, trapped by circumstances. That's all the enemy's bluff, and I've called him on it many times. But conflict remains in my heart. *Was this really God's plan? All the way to forty?* I simply feel sad.

After class, as I talk with Sharyn, I find out she has similar questions. We exchange thoughts. She's by no means a depressed person. *But*, she asks, *where's the hope in it?* We don't need to say it out loud. Although it's natural for most people to assume they will get married someday, there comes a point when you feel like there are no guarantees. And having babies? Well, she's forty-eight.

I talk about redemption, but deep in my soul, I can hardly hear its music over the lament of disappointment. My heart is grieving what the last two decades, those of my youth, never were and never will be. As one unmarried blogger so aptly put it, my story is going to be different. "Is this the story I imagined for myself? Uh, not exactly," she writes. "But it *is* my story, and I believe God *is* intimately, clearly involved in its daily details."[2]

I've felt the disappointment of singleness before, but never to this degree. Now, it feels like a huge loss in my life. Something about turning forty did it, waking me in the middle of the book with the realization that the story really isn't going to turn out the way I thought it would. And though I, too, believe my sovereign God is intimately involved in all the details of the plot, right now the sadness aches, clouds my view of life, blocks the road to redemptive hope. Somehow, I have to get past this disappointment. But it seems like a wall too high to get over and too long to go around.

It's not that I don't know the truth, or that I've lost my faith. I know God will work all things together for my good, according to Romans 8:28. But while I wait for God to work that good according to His purpose, something inside me grieves. In their workshops about dealing with loss, my ministry friends Farrar Moore and Sheryl Cook say it perfectly: *My heart is broken, not my brain.*

Before I can apply the truth I believe, my broken heart must be mended.

BITTERNESS OF SOUL

Her husband adored her, and she adored him. Yet she was disappointed. Hannah longed for a child, but she couldn't seem to conceive.

Her husband longed for a child too. Heirs to pass on the family name, the family property. In fact, Elkanah wanted children so much that, despite his love for Hannah, he married a second wife in hopes that she would be able to conceive.[3] Her name was Penninah.

She was acid to Hannah's wound. Peninnah, overflowing in fertility. Peninnah, having babies with *her* husband. Year after year, another son, another daughter. With each new baby, with the daily sight of those children running around, Hannah's disappointment deepened. She could not ignore her unfulfilled desire to be a mother, the reproach of having to live closely with a rival wife who had received the fulfillment of her own dream.

She could not hide her broken heart, and Peninnah made it obvious that she noticed. Every year that hateful woman taunted Hannah during the annual feast of sacrifice. Parading and showing off her children. Mocking Hannah because she had none.

Every year, Hannah's tears let loose. She got so upset she couldn't eat—could hardly touch the double portion that Elkanah set out especially for her. Set out as a public token of his support and love for her, another thing obviously noticed by Penninah, jealous of Elkanah's favoring Hannah, even though she was the one with children.[4]

Every year, Peninnah's unkindness and Hannah's heartbreak put a damper on the festive mood. Elkanah didn't know how to comfort Hannah, except to hope that his love could make up for her disappointment. But it couldn't. No, it couldn't. It might, however, be the thing that moved Hannah to do something different one particular year, the thing that forced her not to remain in the distress and depression that overwhelmed her.

Whatever the reason, that year something had to change for Hannah. She was at the point where she could bear it no more. So she got up from the table, letting her food grow even colder, and headed straight to the temple.

And there, where she was aware only of God's presence, the closet doors burst open, every emotion tumbling out. The narrator of Samuel chose some very strong words to describe what that looked like: "And she was in bitterness of soul, and prayed to the Lord and wept in anguish" (1 Samuel 1:10, NKJV).

Bitterness of soul. Sounds like a description of a broken heart to me, not to mention words like *anguish* and *weeping*.

Bitterness of soul. That simile for mourning over what never was, that descriptor for deepening layers of disappointment when a circumstance never seems to change. That heartsickness described in Proverbs 13:12, "Hope deferred makes the heart sick, but desire fulfilled is a tree of life" (NAS)—hope meaning *expectation* in the original Hebrew.[5]

And I wonder how many of us have felt that way at least once in our lives? How many of us know the way through bitterness of soul back to hope, or know even what that hope, or expectation, should be?

THE INVITATION

It is the summertime of my fortieth year. I sit down at Betty's table for a cup of tea and one of her amazing berry scones slathered with homemade cream and lemon curd. Time with Betty is always sweet, and so are the treats at her table. Which is a good thing, because today we are talking about disappointment.

"The question isn't whether I have these feelings, but are they dominating my life?" Betty says. "They are invitations to intimacy with the Lord."

Betty is lovely, a mature woman of God. She walked through her own bitterness of soul when her thirty-year marriage ended with an unwanted and painful divorce. And now, years later, she waits for remarriage.

Disappointment, she says, is always in the background for her, pushed to the foreground by different triggers. Triggers, I think, are personal and varied, hitting each of us just the right way at particularly vulnerable moments. Like the news, for Hannah, that Peninnah was pregnant again. Like attending another wedding was for a friend of mine earlier this year. And for me, like hearing about the engagement of another young woman at church who was in elementary school when I started attending as a young woman myself.

When the desire for marriage gets stirred within us, Betty says, we have to realize it is going to hurt. "Accepting the pain that goes with that [desire] is worth it because it creates an opportunity to be intimate with the Lord."

And that's why she calls disappointment an invitation—an invitation to express our feelings in God's presence, to trust Him with the most vulnerable places of our hearts.

It might seem like an unkind way to invite relationship, but it wasn't God's original way. It is His redemptive way in a fallen world. Answering the invitation to share our true feelings with God is the response of faith. In his book, *Disappointment with God*, Philip Yancey writes:

> One bold message in the Book of Job is that you can say anything to God. Throw at him your grief, your anger, your doubt, your bitterness, your betrayal, your disappointment—He can absorb them all. As often as not, spiritual giants of the Bible are shown *contending* with God. They prefer to go away limping, like Jacob, rather than to shut God out. In this respect, the Bible prefigures a tenet of modern psychology: you can't really deny your feelings or make them disappear, so you might as well express them. God can deal with every human response save one. He cannot abide the response I fall back on instinctively: an attempt to ignore Him or treat Him as though He does not exist. That response never once occurred to Job.[6]

Faith is believing that God exists *and* that seeking Him—in *all* circumstances—matters. "And without faith it is impossible to please Him, for he who comes to God must believe that He is, and that He is a rewarder of those who diligently seek Him" (Hebrews 11:6, NKJV).

When we seek God in all circumstances and emotions, we are showing Him our heart's devotion, showing Him we believe He is trustworthy and that it is worthwhile to *us* to stay close to Him even if we don't understand a particular situation. Faith chooses not to shut God out, believing there is a benefit, a reward, in seeking and knowing Him.

Healing for broken hearts is one of those countless rewards. God knows a broken heart cannot be mended until the brokenness is acknowledged and expressed. When I asked one forty-two-year-old never-married woman how she keeps herself from dwelling in a place of disappointment, she said that she acknowledges her feelings. Pretending those feelings don't exist, she said, can cut off relationship with God and other people.

And she's right. Christian counselor Dr. Neil Anderson writes that when we are not emotionally honest and try to cover our feelings to be "spiritual," we become spiritually vulnerable. He quotes 1 Peter 5:7-8: "Cast all your anxiety on Him because He cares for you. Be self-controlled and alert. Your enemy the devil prowls around like a roaring lion looking for someone to devour" (NIV).[7]

And so, God wants to be the first to hear our honest acknowledgement, to see our tears. He wants us to let it all out freely before Him, because He wants to enter into the pain with us. He cares. And our belief that He does—that trust from being deeply known and loved and accepted—is our safe haven, the shield that protects us from the enemy's schemes against us.

King David, the man after God's own heart, knew this. "Trust in Him at all times, O people," he said. "Pour out your heart before Him; God is a refuge for us" (Psalm 62:8, NKJV). This, a tender word about hearts and emotion, from a soldier who often described God with battle terminology: *fortress, stronghold, deliverer*. David knew God's power, which protected him from violence and death when he was physically vulnerable. But he also knew God's heart, which sheltered him with kindness when he was emotionally vulnerable. He goes so far as to say, "The Lord is near to the brokenhearted and saves those who are crushed in spirit" (Psalm 34:18, NAS).

Those feeling emotionally crushed can trust, without shame, the one who Himself was crushed. Jesus was, in Isaiah's words, "despised and forsaken of men, a man of sorrows and acquainted with grief; and like one from whom men hide their face He was despised, and we did not esteem Him" (Isaiah 53:3, NAS).

Yes, even for bitterness of soul, we have Jesus. Jesus, who felt the same losses and emotions we feel, yet never sinned (Hebrews 4:15). Jesus, who wept over the death of His friend Lazarus, who cried in sorrow over Jerusalem's rejection of its Savior. Jesus felt deeply. He spent hours in communion with His Father, expressing His heart, receiving what He needed from the Father's heart. He experienced a close, life-giving relationship with His Father, a deep soul and spirit connection that enabled Him to accomplish the Father's purposes with all grace, peace, and strength. We would do well to emulate the way Jesus handled His emotions.

In their book about dealing with painful experiences, Farrar Moore and Sheryl Cook write, "Jesus and David both modeled for us honest emotional expression…their emotion did not diminish their relationship with God; their expression of emotion enhanced that precious relationship. An emotionless relationship is not really a relationship; there is no place for intimacy void of emotion."[8]

And somehow, Hannah knew this. Hannah was not afraid nor ashamed to sob in front of God, to tell Him how bitterly disappointed she was, and to ask Him to grant the desire of her heart.

THE TURNING POINT

The divorce shocked everybody, devastated her family. Linda struggled with the pain for several years, loneliness and rejection clinging to her.

Finally, one season, something had to change. The downhearted feelings had to go. Linda needed to know why they lingered. "I'm a believer. The Bible says if you need anything to ask of God," she says. "I fasted and asked God to help me understand why I felt the way I did."

She opened her Bible, and God showed her what she needed. Eve's story took on personal meaning when she discovered a phrase she had never seen before in Genesis 3:16: "Your desire shall be for your husband and he shall rule over you" (NKJV).

"It settled me," Linda says. "That was an answer to the way I felt, because of the curse of Eve."

After that, things changed for Linda. She moved forward with her life, no longer stuck in bitterness of soul. God knew what she needed: revelation about the ultimate source of her pain. As she took that pain to the Lord, He responded with His peace.

Linda had reached a turning point in her disappointment, and she found it by seeking the Lord. She experienced the principle that Hannah's story shows us. When Hannah finally finished crying and praying in the temple, she exchanged bitterness of soul for a "face no longer sad" (1 Samuel 1:16).

Hannah had encountered the Father's heart. She traded a victim's pain for a divine daughter's peace, a prisoner's despair for a conqueror's hope. She no longer identified with the reproach of her barrenness. She identified with the God who had gently acknowledged and accepted her. And at the end of the story, she begins to see God's redemptive sovereignty at work. In short, intimacy with God transformed Hannah. It healed her broken heart.

As to how that worked, it is a mystery. Only a few details of Hannah's exchange are provided in the Bible. What we know is that her turning point came through relationship with God. And relationship with the Father involves the Holy Spirit, His presence within us imparting life to our souls. The specifics of that relationship will look different for each one of us, because we are all unique individuals. And so, our turning point moments or seasons, our needs and activities, will all look different, too.

Linda fasted at home; Hannah cried at the temple. I sought a counselor. Annette knelt down by her prayer chair and told God she was at the bottom of her barrel.

"I felt like I was going to die internally," she says, describing her prolonged singleness as the death of a vision and dream for her life. "God absolutely entered in at that moment of my life." He reminded her of Jeremiah 29:11 (NKJV), "For I know the thoughts that I think toward you, says the Lord, thoughts of peace and not of evil, to give you a future and a hope." Over the next year, in numerous supernaturally orchestrated ways, God kept that verse in front of her.

Hannah's reward is available to each of us who seek God with faith in our own bitterness-of-soul experience. No matter when or how those of us burdened with disappointment reach that turning point, we know it has taken place when an encounter with the Lord changes our countenance. He fills our hearts with fresh hope, and our faces are no longer sad.

Based on the sketch of Hannah's experience and the full revelation of God's Word to us now, I've identified a few key elements that characterize turning point encounters with God.

THE WHOLE TRUTH

She was young and pretty. She was newly married to the latest, handsomest, most eligible bachelor of her generation. And as she stood at the front of the church as part of the ministry team that Sunday, anger and resentment toward her pressed against my chest. God's convicting finger pressed harder.

She had never done anything wrong or unkind to me. We didn't even have a relationship. Such irrational and negative feelings were rooted in resenting that she, a much younger woman, had everything I desired and waited long for, but still did not have.

I repented.

We've already talked about how crucial it is to honestly admit and express feelings of disappointment or sadness. In fact, I would say that is the place to start. But those feelings are only part of the whole truth that an honest relationship with God requires. Honesty also acknowledges sin.

As emotions flow from the soul in prayer, the humble heart eventually calms and stills, becoming aware of the mighty, holy, listening God. The heart that truly seeks—not the one that merely vents—opens itself to receiving revelation about sin not yet recognized or confessed. Praying in the Spirit, as well as reading the Word, untangles all the other things mixed up with raw emotion: motivations, jealousies, unbelief, sin. Once again, King David models this kind of emotional honesty. "Purify me with hyssop, and I shall be clean; wash me, and I shall be whiter than snow," he prays in Psalm 51:7 (NKJV).

In the temple, I'd like to believe, Hannah confessed her jealousy and resentment toward Peninnah. She would have been super human not to face those temptations. She came away from her prayer time with peace, a sign she was right with God, cleansed from whatever He had revealed was wrong in her heart. And this is especially important where bitterness of soul is concerned.

"If we don't process that bitterness of soul, it becomes a seed of bitterness," says my friend Betty. "If there is anything in my heart that accuses God, that's what needs to be expressed and brought before Him."

Seeds of bitterness, not confessed and dealt with, are an opportunity for the devil to water them with lies about God and about ourselves until they become roots of bitterness. That convicting Sunday morning was not the first time I had begrudged that young woman for her "success." But it was the first day I fully acknowledged the sin in my heart. If I did not confess and deal with it then, how many more lies about her and my own situation would I continue to let into my mind? As Ephesians 5:26-27 says, "Be angry, and yet do not sin; do not let the sun go down on your anger, and do not give the devil an opportunity" (NAS). Negative emotion not brought before the Lord on a regular basis—a *daily* basis, according to this Scripture—piles up, water upon seed, yielding the fruit of the flesh in our lives.

Without realizing it, we can easily believe lies that are hidden under our natural feelings of disappointment. An honest time before the Lord in repentance and humility is also a good time to ask Him to show us what is true and what is false. For example, the lie that God is not good, or that life is never going to be as good as it would be if we were married. Or the belief that we are unlovable or unworthy—an old maid. As God brings a lie to light, look for the scriptural truth that replaces it. Truths such as "Oh, taste and see that the Lord is good; blessed is the man who trusts in Him!" (Psalm 34:8, NKJV) and "See how great a love the Father has bestowed on us, that we would be called children of God; and such we are" (1 John 3:1, NAS).

Suppose Hannah saw herself as a victim for all those years—a victim of her closed womb, of her society's emphasis on women as child-bearers, of Peninnah's torment. If she did, she had to get rid of that lie before she could pray in faith that God would give her a son.

Roots of bitterness block belief. And unbelief, besides being a sin, is what keeps us from expecting and experiencing the full redemption of every loss in our lives, which is very closely tied to the next key for experiencing a turning point.

WHAT DO I LOOK FOR?

For Lisa, bitterness of soul hit when she turned thirty. She had determined that she was finally ready to be married. But she was still single, and she had what she called "blue times."

"I wouldn't call it depressed," she says. "But I would get very sad. I would cry for a week or two weeks every night going to sleep. It was all about not being married."

After a while the blues would go away, and she would feel better. But they always returned. After about a year and a half of intermittent blues, Lisa had enough. She needed a turning point.

"I just got on my knees and said, 'Lord this is not right,'" she says. She wanted to live the abundant life He promised, to know His plan for her life. *You have to show me how to get over this and how to not live this way,* she prayed.

"He showed me He's sovereign," she says. "He showed me, 'I knew where you're going to be this very minute when I knit you together in your mother's womb...I am taking care of you. This is exactly what I have planned for you.' That gave me peace, and I never had any time like that again."

From that encounter with God, Lisa felt an assurance that she would be married, even if she had to wait until she was fifty years old. (She didn't. God blessed her with marriage in her early forties.) From that point forward, Lisa determined to enjoy her life and prepare for marriage.

Lisa received a specific promise from God during her encounter with Him. It came through the Holy Spirit, and she had such assurance that she believed it until it was fulfilled.

And such was Hannah's experience. Who knows what the Holy Spirit whispered to her heart and whether she felt that He promised her a son. What we do know is that she heard the voice of the priest. He was, at that time, the mediator between God and His people. After watching Hannah (first mistaking her for a crazy drunk), Eli, the priest, spoke a word of confirmation; a promise, perhaps, that God would answer her prayer: "Go in peace, and may the God of Israel grant your petition which you have asked of Him" (1 Samuel 1:17, NKJV).

After that, Hannah went back to the table and ate her meal. She left her disappointment in the temple and faced her life with a new hope. She had received something from the Lord in her moment of need.

And that is the next key: receiving revelation. If we're going to move forward in life, as Linda did, as Annette did, as Lisa did, we have to have something to go on. Something to look for. Something to hold on to. We need a personal promise for our lives.

Receiving promises from the Lord begins with believing the truth He has already revealed in His Word. Truth about who we are in Him and the kind of lives He intends for us to live. Those truths combat the lies we accepted. I think about Annette's turning point by her prayer chair, which occurred many years ago. Now almost fifty, Annette is still unmarried, but she still believes the promise of a future and a hope that came out of her encounter that day.

Some of us receive specific promises about marriage and motherhood, which we can reasonably expect to be confirmed in some way. Some of us do not receive those specifics. The idea is not to look for a promise of marriage in every verse, in every flutter of leaf or mysterious whisper of wind. The point is to receive what only God knows we need, the revelation that will bring peace and healing to our hearts.

The goal is to know Jesus. To hear, to sense, to know His answer in the deep places of our spirits that go beyond words.

How do we get to that place with Him? "We have to start with believing," says Bible teacher Toni Kline, speaking one Sunday morning. "The chief duty of our soul is to believe. There is nothing else that is more important for our soul than to believe." We have to believe in all that Jesus is.

Toni's text was John 14:1: "Let not your heart be troubled; you believe in God, believe also in Me" (NKJV). She explained that it's as if Jesus is saying, *Believe in who I am as a person. Don't just believe things about me; that's very different from believing in me.*

We must believe in Jesus as God and Savior, as Redeemer and Love. As all-sufficient and all-powerful. We must believe He is more than able to meet every need in our lives, that He is the one in whom all confidence can be placed. It is this belief in Jesus that enables us to receive the revelation we need to get through and beyond whatever circumstance is troubling our hearts.

"Believing was the condition of receiving the revelation and enjoying the reality of the promise He was getting ready to communicate to [the disciples]. If we don't believe, we will not get a revelation," Toni says. "We'll have no capacity to receive a revelation from Him. We'll have no capacity to see a future, we'll have no capacity to believe in the promise of His Word."[9]

Belief in Jesus' character and goodness—and His sovereignty—is essential to turning the corner from disappointment's darkness to hope's light. Hannah believed that God's power could, and would, overcome the circumstances that she felt powerless to change. She believed that, against all medical and physical odds, He could make the barren womb conceive. She didn't turn to other gods or to concubines, looking for something or someone else in which to place her faith. He alone was her hope. And He made good on His promise.

Whatever promise Jesus speaks to us in the secret place of our relationship with Him, our faith in His promise flows from our belief in who He is. As a result, we leave that place with hope and the ability to move forward in peace.

Peace—even if our circumstances do not change, because He Himself is our peace. And peace because we have discovered and experienced more of Him personally, entrusting our lives to His care.

OPEN HANDS

Her husband died a martyr, murdered by the people he came to evangelize. She was in her twenties at the time, and their first child was a baby. Later in life, after many years as a single mother, she married again. And then her second husband died, a painfully drawn out death, from cancer. So Elisabeth Elliot knows what she is talking about:

> I have tried to explain it sometimes to people who are lonely and longing for love. "Give it to Jesus," I say. The loneliness itself is material for sacrifice. The very longings themselves can be offered to Him who understands perfectly. The transformation into something He can use for the good of others takes place only when the offering is put into His hands. What will He do with these offerings? Nevermind. He knows what to do.[10]

In a nutshell, Elliot is saying, surrender. Surrender the dying dream, the expectations unfulfilled. Offer them as a sacrifice to Him, leaving them in His hands for safe keeping. Offer them with a sacrifice of praise, for this is reasonable worship. And it is the fruit of a true encounter with God, the evidence of a turning point on the path of disappointment.

Hannah's story exemplifies this, too. As Hannah poured out her heart to God, she didn't stop desiring to have a child. Instead, she realized that even this God-given desire, perhaps the one most cherished in her heart, needed to be presented to God as worship. That's why she made a vow that if He gave her a son, she would return him to the Lord as a Nazirite—he would be set apart, as Samson was.

For Hannah, this would mean leaving her little boy in the care of the priest and seeing him only once a year. That sacrifice had already been made in her heart before the desired child arrived. The dream had been surrendered, even before it was received.

When God gave Hannah the child she prayed for, she and Elkanah brought a bull, some flour, and a jug of wine with them on Samuel's dedication day at the temple. Their offerings were in accordance with the Law, but there was one commandment they did not follow, exactly.

In Exodus 13, as the first Passover was about to take place, God commanded His people through Moses to sanctify every firstborn child—the one who opened the womb. This process of dedication to the Lord meant *redeeming* the child at the temple with a monetary offering—essentially, buying him back from the Lord, to whom he belonged (Numbers 18:15-16). But the Scripture doesn't say Hannah and Elkanah brought money to redeem Samuel.

Instead of leaving an offering at the temple and taking their son home, they left their child at the temple, as Hannah said, "that he may appear before the Lord and stay there forever" (1 Samuel 1:22, NKJV).

Samuel became the living sacrifice of his parents. And to me he pictures the reasonable, spiritual service of worship that all the

Lord's redeemed children, the apostle Paul says, must do: present our bodies a living and holy sacrifice (Romans 12:1).

We can do it because it's the same sacrifice the Redeemer made first, the one He made for us. The sacrifice that redeemed us, that bought us back from sin's curse, the enemy's power, and the fallen world's bitterness of soul.

That's not to say the sacrifice came easy for Jesus, even though He was sent to be the Redeemer of the world. I considered this one morning as I read from Hebrews:

> In the days of His flesh [Jesus] offered up definite, special petitions [for that which He not only wanted but needed] and supplications with strong crying and tears to Him Who was [always] able to save Him [out] from death, and He was heard because of His reverence toward God [His godly fear, His piety, in that He shrank from the horrors of separation from the bright presence of the Father]. (Hebrews 5:7, AMP)

Going to the cross was not easy for Jesus, for more reasons than the horrific pain He would experience. Elsewhere in Scripture it says He became a curse for us (Galatians 3:13). The source of purity became filthy, shameful, dirty, and separated from God the Father, a very part of Himself.

As Jesus cried out in the garden of Gethsemane, it's as if the Father whispered to Him, *Are you willing to go through this for me?* And Jesus said, *Yes,* though He sweated great drops of blood at the thought. Sweating blood is a rare but real medical condition that occurs when capillaries burst beneath the skin when a person is under extreme emotional stress. After describing this condition, one theologian writes:

> From these factors, it is evident that even before Jesus endured the torture of the cross, He suffered far beyond what most of us will ever suffer. His penetrating awareness of the heinous nature of sin, its destructive and deadly effects, the sorrow and heartache that it inflicts, and the extreme measure necessary to deal with it, make the passion of Christ beyond all comprehension.[11]

Even though it went against His emotional and physical desires, Jesus surrendered His will to the Father's. The Father could only accomplish His purpose through the Son's obedience even to death. And this, too, was reasonable worship.

The writer of Hebrews speaks about making a sacrifice of praise to God. Sacrifice and surrender are not necessarily easy or emotionally pleasant. But when done, God's purpose can be fulfilled, even His plan for us to live victoriously in all circumstances. "Worship was the foundation of man's being and potential. Thus, God's redemptive program is founded in worship," writes Dr. Jack Hayford. As a result, "The true worshiper is not ruled by death, neither by its force nor its fear. He has dominion over it."[12]

As we open our hands in surrender, as we lift them in worship, we let go of disappointment's power over us. Our emotions may not change immediately, but, like Jesus, we will be able to focus on the joy set before us (Hebrews 12:2). The victim's chains fall from our open hands, and new strength empowers us to forge ahead as more than a conqueror.

Offering ourselves to His service, we are ready to take hold of a fresh revelation, ready to let Him accomplish His purpose in our present circumstances, even in singleness. We are ready to say, *Though this circumstance is less than desirable to me, I am willing to go through it with You, for Your glory.*

As Jesus showed us, it is the sacrifice of worship that makes redemption possible.

WHAT NEVER DISAPPOINTS

My friend Betty tells the story of a shopping trip that triggered the pain of losing her marriage. She was looking through the racks at a department store when a special song came on through the intercom. It had been *their* song.

It transported Betty to a long-ago evening when she was cooking dinner with her husband. She could smell the food on the stove; she could feel his arms around her as they danced to that song in the kitchen. She felt afresh the sadness of losing that special relationship with him.

Betty needed a turning point in that moment, lest her shopping trip be cut short and her day ruined. She saw an opportunity for intimacy with her Lord, the one who knew her heart deeply, who invited her to come to Him with her pain.

So she did. She slipped away to the fitting room and took a few minutes to pray through both her past and present emotions and to receive a healing touch from the Lord as He met her there. After acknowledging her emotions, Betty reaffirmed the truth about who she is in Christ, and her peace returned.

After that she was able to go back to her shopping and focus her attention on the very important task at hand—finding the perfect bargain.[13]

For many of us, different circumstances will trigger disappointment even after we've turned the corner. It may still linger in the background, or it may not. Whatever the case, when we take the time to seek God in every one of these moments, we experience daily turning points that take us back to the thing that never disappoints.

> And not only that, but we also glory in tribulations, knowing that tribulation produces perseverance; and perseverance, character, and character, hope. Now hope does not disappoint, because the love of God has been poured out in our hearts by the Holy Spirit who was given to us (Romans 5:3-5, NKJV).

Hope.

Hope, which comes from allowing God to shape our character through the very thing that brought us disappointment.

Hope, which is expectation. An expectation of what?

King David once asked, then answered, that very question. "But now, Lord, what do I look for? My hope is in You" (Psalm 39:7, NIV).

And in the midst of my turning point season, this was God's revelation to me: Hope is Jesus. I look for Him. I wait for Him. I expect *Him* in every moment, every day, every season. Jesus, and all that I believe and know Him to be.

When I expect Jesus, I understand that it is through my deepening relationship with Him that He redeems the emotions of loss. I realize that He alone—not a changed circumstance, not marriage, not motherhood, not singleness—can rescue me from all heartsickness, from every grief. He alone can take every experience and circumstance of loss and turn them into gain—both my gain, and, somehow, His.

For that's what redemption means.

NOTES

1. Amy Carmichael, "Rose From Brier," in *Mountain Breezes: The Collected Poems of Amy Carmichael* (Ft. Washington, PA: Christian Literature Crusade, 1999), 294.
2. Amy, "Discouragement and Things Made New," *Fast. Pray.* (blog), June 18, 2012, http://fastpray.wordpress.com/2012/06/18/discouragement-things-made-new/.
3. Matthew Henry, *Matthew Henry Commentary on the Whole Bible (Complete)*, "1 Samuel 1," BibleStudyTools.com, accessed May 17, 2011, http://biblestudytools.com/commentaries/matthew-henry-complete/1-samuel/1.html?p=2.
4. Ibid.
5. James Strong, L.L.D., S.T.D., *New Strong's Concise Dictionary of the Words in the Hebrew Bible* in *The New Strong's Exhaustive Concordance of the Bible* (Nashville: Thomas Nelson, 1995), 151.
6. Philip Yancey, *Disappointment with God* (Grand Rapids, MI: Zondervan, 1988), 263.
7. Neil T. Anderson, *Victory Over the Darkness* (Ventura, CA: Regal Books, 1990), 196.
8. Farrar Moore with Sheryl Cook and Betty Plank, *From Hurt to Hope* (Nashville: Caring Resources, 2007), 26-27.
9. Toni Kline, "Ministering Like Jesus: Believe," (sermon, New Song Christian Fellowship, Spring Hill, TN, August 6, 2012).
10. Elisabeth Elliot, *Passion and Purity* (Grand Rapids, MI: Fleming H. Revell, 1984), 65.
11. Dave Miller, Ph.D., "Did Jesus Sweat Blood?", *Apologetics Press* (website), 2004, http://www.apologeticspress.org.

12. Jack Hayford, *Worship His Majesty* (Ventura: Regal Books, 2000), 36, 42.

13. Farrar Moore with Sheryl Cook and Betty Plank, *From Hurt to Hope* (Nashville: Caring Resources, 2007), 101-102. Betty has also told this story with additional details at HOPE Workshops sponsored by Caring Resources.

Part 2

Redemption

"Who doesn't want the new thing? The past not to hurt. The weight loss. The anger to go away. There is a billion dollar industry that exists to bring us forward in personal growth, to achieve personal best, to gather personal fortune. To go from point A to point B. And yet two thousand years ago, Jesus said... I make all things new-come follow me."

- Kathy Troccoli[1]

– Chapter 5 –

Being Rescued *from* Loss

It is mid-summer of my thirty-second year, and I am spending my vacation at my parents' house many states away. On this particular sunny afternoon, I'm keenly aware of my singleness.

The whole family has gathered together for a picnic. Two of my sisters are married, and there is the recent excitement of babies and pregnancies; my sisters aglow with motherhood, my parents alive with grandparent-hood. I watch the family activity around me, the happiness palpable. I miss the husband and child I don't yet have.

I sit in a lawn chair, loneliness stirred—not because I don't belong to my biological family, but because I don't belong to a partner with whom I can become my own family. I watch my three-year-old nephew playing on the deck, running around, and then, before you know it, tripping and falling. He isn't really hurt, but he cries. I pick him up and cuddle him on my lap.

A few minutes pass, and I know he is fine. But he refuses to loosen his embrace around me, snuggling his face deeper against my chest. I'm secretly glad and hold him tightly. I bask in his warmth, the closeness of his little red head against me, his child's response to my rarely-sought maternal instincts. I don't move, don't want to break the moment, don't want him to let go.

And the moment lasts, stretches into ten quiet minutes under the fluttering poplar trees, rich minutes of intimacy and grace, of physical and emotional affection. My nephew lifts his face, looks into mine, and covers it with kisses—both cheeks, forehead. Wherever he can reach. Then I let him down, and he goes back to his playing.

I sit still, stunned, receiving and receiving, feeling the Lord fill loss's vacuum with something very, very good. I sense God's presence and care, full and real, His acknowledgement of my loneliness. I see how He has reached into my moment of loss and brought gain out of it. Gain for me, which also somehow met the need of a little boy.

I recognize it as redemption.

THE SEED OF LOSS'S UNDOING

Pain in childbirth. Your husband shall rule over you. In toil you shall work the ground. To dust you shall return.

How those words must have reverberated throughout the silent, sin-struck garden! How chilly she must have felt, Eve—standing in her fig leaves, shame-faced, listening to the curses her disobedience produced.

Disappointment. Hardship. Loss.

Life as it was not meant to be.

The overarching loss in all of it was relationship with God, who would no longer walk with Man and Woman in the garden. This loss, the one that undermines all others, left a black hole in every person's soul, left us floundering for identity, love, hope, and life itself. Ever since, humanity has desperately longed and cried out for redemption of that nameless void, that unidentified restless and dissatisfied place. And so people seek things, experiences, love—and in today's society, especially romantic love, as the answer to that deepest place of need. Writing about humanity's need for and approach to love, Dr. Timothy Keller quotes from a Pulitzer Prize-winning work by the secular cultural anthropologist Ernest Becker:

> After all, what is it that we want when we elevate the love partner to this position? We want to be rid of our faults, of our feeling of nothingness. We want to be justified, to know our existence has not been in vain. We want redemption—nothing less. Needless to say, human partners cannot give this.[2]

No one can redeem the losses of the Fall, except God Himself. And so, even before God had listed the consequences of sin for Man and Woman, He planted a seed of hope. In what must have sounded like a riddle to Eve, He said of the serpent, who had started it all, "And I will put enmity between you and the woman, and between your seed and her seed; He shall bruise you on the head, and you shall bruise him on the heel" (NAS) or, as the NIV puts it, "he will crush your head, and you will strike his heel" (Genesis 3:15).

Scholars have a wonderful theological term for this verse: *protoevangelium*. Protoevangelium is the first announcement of the gospel, the first promise that a Redeemer would come. The first prophecy of redemption of all that wasn't meant to be.

The most common word for *redeem* in the Old Testament means "to rescue, ransom, to purchase, to buy back." In the New Testament, *redeem* has a similar meaning—"to buy up for oneself, to ransom."[3] But there's another way *redeem* is used in the New Testament, and that is "to rescue from loss" or "improve opportunity."[4]

Jesus ransomed us, bought our freedom from death with His own life, rescued us from the losses incurred by sin, and improved everything—our status, outlook, potential, and destiny—with His resurrection life. In Jesus, everything is better. Everything is made new.

Eve could not have guessed all of that. One of the most fascinating things to me about the *protoevangelium* is this: It declares that Woman, who was first to make a choice contrary to God's will, would become an integral part of how God planned to accomplish redemption. In fact, He couldn't do it without her, because centuries later He would need her to make the divine human through childbirth—redeeming even that cursed female pain.

God announced a day of resurrection even as He pronounced the consequences of death over the world. And this is God's pattern woven into human destiny through His sovereign love—the everyday work of improving our opportunities, of rescuing loss from being only empty loss. Songwriter Jason Gray articulates it beautifully when speaking about his song, "Everything Sad is Coming Untrue":

> ...somehow, even right now in the face of the saddest that we see, the seeds of its undoing are sown. In fact, they were sown the day the body of Jesus, like a seed himself, was laid in the ground. What took root on Easter is the undoing of the curse, and it is flowering all around us if we have eyes to see it.[5]

If we have eyes to see it.

As Christians, we understand by faith that our souls are redeemed and will be fully redeemed when Jesus returns to earth for His people. But while we wait for the eternal redemption of all that wasn't meant to be, we can expect that resurrection life to be at work in every part of our lives on earth, including prolonged singleness. Because His redemption reaches even to that.

Whatever losses we experience, Jesus rescues them from being merely losses when we walk with Him, keeps the situation from staying in the red. He turns them into gain, into something better than what they are in the natural. This gain-from-loss is the story told over and over in the Bible. It is Abraham's Isaac. It is Manoah's Samson and Hannah's Samuel. It is Ruth's Boaz and Naomi's Obed. It is Rachel's Joseph.

And it is Joseph's not-meant-to-be life of mishap after mishap—rejection, slavery, betrayal, imprisonment—that led to prominence and position, which eventually brought his hateful brothers to their knees before him. Reflecting on Joseph's life, Philip Yancey says this:

> Through all his trials, Joseph learned to trust: not that God would prevent hardship, but that he would redeem even the hardship. Choking back tears, Joseph tried to explain his faith to his murderous brothers: "You intended to harm me, but God intended it for good…"[6]

For whose good was this redemption? Surely Joseph's, but not just his. The gain that came from his loss benefited so many more. Writer and pastor Robert Morgan expresses it so well:

> Under the wise administration of Joseph, Egypt was saved from famine, the Hebrew people were saved from starvation, his father's house were spared from drought, the Jewish people were placed in an incubator where they would multiply into a great nation, and the messianic seed was preserved and protected as it wended its way through the generations toward the ultimate birth of the Savior of the world.[7]

The Savior's Church is still reaping the redemption of Joseph's losses. Redemption is at the very heart of God's plan for us, and it's ours to look for.

LOOKING FOR REDEMPTION

How long did she cry when her husband died?

It had only been seven years—years that passed swiftly, sweetly. Years now gone. A marriage now lost. And Anna was still young. This is not the way she saw her story going.

But one day, after the crying stopped, or maybe because it wouldn't stop, Anna reached her turning point. She came to a decision, and her life was forever changed.

She would make herself a living sacrifice at the temple, serving God with prayer and fasting, morning and evening. She would live in hope, in expectation. And what she expected was Redemption.

All we have of Anna's story are the few lines scratched down in Luke's gospel. He doesn't mention whether Anna had any children. Since she ministered to God day and night in the temple, she probably lived in one of its rooms, perhaps benefitting from a ministry to widows.[8] It doesn't seem likely she could have spent so much time in the temple if she were raising children, or that she would have been there as an old lady instead of at the homes of her grown children.

For she was present at the temple always, day after day, year after year, until she was an old woman the day Mary and Joseph walked in with their firstborn Son.

The day that Anna saw with her own eyes the promised Redemption.

Never mind that her circumstances hadn't changed.

Though Luke gave us but a sketch of Anna's life, what he tells us shows the richness and depth of her walk with God. He identifies her as a prophetess, someone who received and delivered messages from God, someone who lived in close relationship with Him. When Mary and Joseph came into the temple to dedicate their child, Jesus, Anna knew right away He was the Messiah, the promise her people had been waiting for: "And coming in that instant she gave thanks to the Lord, and spoke of Him to all those who looked for redemption in Jerusalem" (Luke 2:38, NKJV).

How did she know He was the one in the "instant" that Luke described? Yes, she was a prophetess, but no doubt, she had sowed prayer and faith into this hope of hers. Perhaps that's what she prayed for in the temple all those years. She backed her faith and expectation with her spiritual activity, and it gave her eyes to see Redemption when He came.

One female writer, imagining what Anna's life might have been like, portrays her as a childless woman who is sensitive to the things of the Lord, drawn to the temple even as a child. In the writer's fictitious account, Anna asks this question when her husband dies: "Were all my hopes and dreams just foolishness? Lord, I even felt that it was your desire to give me a son. Was I mistaken?"

Years later, when she is old, God answers her this way: "I have heard your prayers for many years. Even as a young woman, I heard your petitions asking me for a son. Today I have come to tell you that you will indeed have a son. This is not a child who will come through your womb, but a child born through the years of the travailing of your spirit. This baby is the promised Messiah and His birth will be the culmination of your life's work."[9]

Anna's life's work—what was it? She was a widow. Childless, perhaps. She had lost the social status of being in a family, married with children. But God had a purpose to accomplish through her life despite her circumstances—yes, maybe even *because* of them. Would she have spent so much time in prayer and communion with God otherwise? Would she have been one of the first to recognize and announce His arrival?

Matthew Henry writes this about Anna's work as announcer of Redemption's coming:

> She *spoke of him to all them* that believed the Messiah would come, and with him l*ooked for redemption in Jerusalem.* Redemption was the thing wanted, waited for, and wished for; redemption *in Jerusalem*, for thence the *word of the Lord was to go forth*, Isaiah 2:3. Some there were in Jerusalem that *looked for redemption*; yet but a few, for Anna, it should seem, had acquaintance with all them that were joint-expectants with her of the Messiah; she knew where to find them, or they where

> to find her, and she told them all the good news, that she had seen the Lord; and it was great news, this of his birth now, as afterwards that of his resurrection.[10]

Redemption was the thing wanted, waited for, and wished for.

Redemption is the presence and person of Jesus Christ, showing up in a moment, a season, or a lifetime of loss. And when Jesus shows up, everything gets better.

BETTER THAN IT LOOKS

Dismal, her view of the future.

Nothing left for her here, with husband and sons all dead. No grandchildren, no property, no prospects. Nothing left to do now but return to her homeland.

So that's what Naomi decided to do. And she wanted to do it alone, without obligating her foreign daughters-in-law to travel with her, awaiting the destitute widow's fate.

Yes, a seemingly dismal fate it would be. In Israel, Naomi's homeland, foreign women were not generally regarded as eligible for marriage.[11] Even the redemptive levirate law of marriage, in which a deceased man's brother or close relative—known as the kinsman redeemer—married his widow to carry on his family line, didn't seem a possibility. Even if Naomi had any marriage prospects, she would never have more sons whom her daughters-in-law could marry.

And without marriage, they could inherit nothing. Though widows in other nearby countries had the right to inherit land, in

Israel, they did not.[12] The only exception was redemption through levirate marriage, when the relative who married a widow inherited the land of her late husband. If the family was poor and couldn't support the widow, or there was no available or willing kinsman redeemer, there was no alternative.[13]

Besides all that, there was the drab widow's garments they had to wear, hiding their social and financial status from no one (see Gen. 38:14-19).

No, Naomi insisted, her daughters-in-law would not come with her, for their own good. But something happened that Naomi didn't expect: Ruth refused to stay behind. She traveled alongside her mother-in-law, ready to face an unknown future with her own genuine faith in God. Naomi did not know it, but when her son married Ruth the Moabitess, the seed of undoing was planted in the family's yet unknown future of loss.

So the women set off for Israel, two widows empty-handed. Maybe Naomi thought being home would bring her comfort, make her glad again. But when they arrived, any joy dissipated as she felt afresh the sorrow of her loss. The old land—it had been *theirs*. The familiar scenes—places where her sons had played. Her returning to it all—*alone*. [14]

The widow's fate is suddenly more hers, more appalling, back here with her old friends and relatives. The reproach of widowhood, of loss, rushes in. "Do not call me Naomi," she says. "Call me Mara, for the Almighty has dealt very bitterly with me. I went out full, and the Lord has brought me home again empty. Why do you call me Naomi, since the Lord has testified against me, and the Almighty has afflicted me?" (Ruth 1:20-21, NKJV).

Why and how did she end up a widow, bereft of children? She wasn't even a grandmother. Her given name, which means *pleasant*, no longer applied. *Mara*, which means *bitter*, made more sense. And she felt God could have prevented it all.

How surprising then, as the weeks unfold, that Ruth happened to glean wheat in the field of Boaz—one who might qualify as kinsman redeemer. Naomi dropped subtle hints about him to Ruth, not previously imagining the possibility, not wanting to stir false hope. Perhaps if Ruth remained in Boaz's field as she suggested, a relationship between them might begin.[15] It was just the beginning of barley harvest in March. By the end of the season, it would be May[16]—plenty of time for a connection to form.

And, perhaps, it was plenty of time for Naomi to work through her own bitterness of soul. The Scripture records her bitterness, but it doesn't say when Naomi reached her turning point. Absorbed with her own pain and circumstances that weren't meant to be, Naomi lamented her losses to her friends without even a mention of Ruth's kindness and companionship.

But by the beginning of the threshing season, Naomi has changed. Her concern is for Ruth, and she wants her to benefit from the law of levirate marriage. Scholar and teacher Rabbi Yitzchak Etshalom says, "The text recognizes Naomi's stake in the success of this mission; yet the first concern which motivates Naomi seems to be Ruth's welfare—a sure sign that Naomi is 'back to her good old self.'"[17] The indication is that Naomi had processed her disappointment and was ready to respond with faith to God's sovereignty in her unexpected circumstances.

So she kept her ears open for any talk of Boaz. Ruth kept to Boaz's field all spring, through the barley harvest, and stayed through the wheat harvest as well, when the barley was left to dry before threshing. June arrived, and barley threshing was in full swing.[18] When that season ended, Ruth might not have a reason to remain in his field. Naomi decided it was time to act.

"My daughter, shall I not seek security for you, that it may be well with you? Now is not Boaz our kinsman, with whose maids you were? Behold, he winnows barley at the threshing floor tonight" (Ruth 3:1-2).

Ruth took Naomi's advice and headed down to the threshing floor, following her instructions to lie down at his feet. When Boaz awakened in the night and saw her, she explained why she was there: "I am Ruth, your maidservant. Take your maidservant under your wing, for you are a close relative" (Ruth 3:9, NKJV).

And Boaz did. He first had to square things away with a closer relative than himself, but in very short order, the two kinsmen had a discussion in the presence of the city elders. Boaz purchased the land of Naomi's husband, redeeming his family property and lineage. And Ruth became his wife with the purchase of the land.

Ruth's story is one of multi-layered redemption, one we will revisit in chapter seven. Her redemptive circumstances are only possible because of Naomi; but, as it turned out, Naomi's redemption was only possible through Ruth. Naomi didn't gain a husband or the ability to bear more children, but she did gain a new family through Ruth.

Grandmother, she would be called. No, something better—*mother of a newborn son*. For Ruth's firstborn son was, in fact, regarded as Naomi's own child, heir of her late husband and sons through Ruth's levirate marriage.

> Then the women said to Naomi, "Blessed is the Lord who has not left you without a redeemer today, and may his name become famous in Israel. May he also be to you a restorer of life and a sustainer of your old age; for your daughter-in-law, who loves you and is better to you than seven sons, has given birth to him." Then Naomi took the child and laid him in her lap, and became his nurse. The neighbor women gave him a name, saying, "A son has been born to Naomi!" (Ruth 4:14-19).

Naomi's dismal future turned out to be better than she thought it could be—so much better. God had so much more for Naomi than a widow's loss. So much more.

And that is the kind of redemption God plans for us—so much more.

SO MUCH MORE

She was forty years old and never married. Circumstantially, everything seemed to be working against her. She'd been in the same city for sixteen years without meeting the right guy.

And the things people said. They could be so negative about marriage, about marrying older. *It's all hard work and adjustment because you're set in your ways. You won't really know what he's like until you're married, and then…*

Then what? It all goes down hill from there?

Even so, she wanted to be married. *But who's left for me?* It seemed like there was a shortage of potential men. And seemingly less possible now, the idea that she would find a man who had saved himself for her, as she had for him.

"You know what I got?" she told me several years later, as a married woman. "A guy who was a virgin, who loved God with all His heart…who loves me more than I can imagine. I kept waiting for him to get bored and move on [while we were dating]. Every day he loves me more."

She thought, *How did I get you? How did God save you for me?* As if her husband wasn't enough, her experience of marriage at an older age was better than people had predicted. "What they didn't tell me was it'll be a lot of fun because you're working on the same goal, an environment you want to be in," she said. "It's a joy, not a drudgery."

For this woman, the marriage that redeemed her singleness was so much more than her circumstances or peers led her to expect. Her passion, her excitement, still stirs encouragement in me: "I'm here to tell you this is the best thing that ever happened to me and the easiest—when God brings you together, it can happen that way. [My husband] is the greatest blessing God has ever given me, and we both feel that way."

Can it really be that good?

In Christ, it can. No matter what the redemption is, what the circumstances are. Another woman, somewhere in her late forties, Peggy, is not yet married. But the quality of God's redemptive work in her life stirs no less zeal.

"I've gotten to know Him better than I ever could have if I were married," she says. "That's where the redemption part is for me."

As a younger woman, Peggy dated a man for nine years. But not all was as it should have been in the relationship. "When the Lord broke it off, that's when I turned around," she says, "when I learned to study my Bible." She had been very dependent and focused on this man, and losing that relationship opened the door to deeper personal and spiritual growth.

"There's so much more for me," she says. "I found myself; I found my Savior. I found the relationship that was more important."

As she spoke of her walk with the Lord, Peggy referred to Him as "my Christ."

My Christ. What she wouldn't trade for the relationship she lost, or the marriage she doesn't have.

My Christ. His way, His method of redemption, His orchestrating of circumstances, cannot be predicted. If we have a promise for marriage, we must hold to it in faith. But regardless, Jesus has *so much more* in store. A glorious purpose to fulfill. We are His, and He is ours. His redemptive work and purposes in our lives will be as unique and individual as we are.

But, if we cooperate with Him, His redemption will always include a more intimate relationship with Him. Because His is the more important relationship.

Just ask Job. He endured more loss than many of us ever will, yet stood overwhelmed in God's presence at his most destitute point. Early on, Job said this: "For I know my Redeemer lives…and after my skin is destroyed, this I know that in my flesh I shall see God, whom I shall see for myself" (Job 19:25-27, NKJV). Job had put his hope in his Redeemer, whom he believed he would see one day after his earthly body was dead and gone. But, perhaps to his surprise, he learned that God was also the Redeemer of hardship and losses of life on earth. For there in the dust and ashes, there bereft of his ten children, his wealth, and his health—right there, God met him, in a storm of all places.

I had heard about you before, but now I have seen you with my own eyes.

These words, his conclusion after that encounter storm-side (Job 42:5, NLT), before God restored everything to Job. Now, he could say, he truly *knew* God—the *so much more* of relationship.

After that came God's physical and circumstantial redemption, also so much more. Here's how the writer put it: "Now the Lord blessed the latter days of Job more than his beginning" (Job 42:12, NKJV). God restored 14,000 sheep for the 7,000 he lost. Six thousand camels for the 3,000 lost, and 1,000 donkeys for the 500 lost.

And then, ten more children: seven sons for the seven he lost and three daughters for the three he lost. While those ten children could never replace the individuals he had loved, each one served as a personal reminder that God acknowledged and cared about that loss. God had given him a family once again. I find it interesting that the writer took the time to name Job's three daughters of redemption and describe their great beauty. They were no ordinary women and even received an inheritance along with their brothers (Job 42:14-15).

Job's loss was deep. But when redemption came, it went deeper, reached farther. Joseph would say the same—Joseph, whose humiliation, servitude, and rejection brought him the opportunity to save his nation, not to mention reconciliation with his family, years later. And so would Hannah, or Manoah, whose sons of barrenness brought more than a baby to a couple. These babies grew into men who played a key part in God's plan for their nation.

Singer-songwriter Marty McCall recorded these lyrics in a simple, beautiful song, and how I love them:

Our loss goes deep / Your comfort goes deeper …
Our wounds go deep / Your healing goes deeper
Our lies are broad / Your truth is broader
Our sins grow fast / Your grace grows faster
Our night is long / Your day is longer, longer, longer[19]

In Jesus, everything is better. And in the words of Jason Gray, it feels like this:

In the way the shadows hide / When the sun begins to rise
And in the way the world comes alive / At the first hint of spring
The frozen rivers run / The death of winter comes undone
Whispers of Kingdom Come / When the bluebird sings …
When we learn to live again / And let forgiveness win
There's no wound that love won't mend / And finally redeem …
Everything that I thought I knew…
Everything sad is coming untrue.[20]

The permanence of sadness and loss is the thing that is coming untrue. Regardless of how God redeems our singleness—with marriage or with something else, or with a combination of many things, we can be confident in knowing it will be so much more because it comes from "Him who is able to do exceedingly abundantly above all that we ask or think, according to the power that works in us" (Ephesians 3:20, NKJV).

RECOGNIZING REDEMPTION

It may come in a moment or a season. It may correspond to an emotion or an experience, a place or a person. Or persons.

Redemption.

I don't pretend to know all the ways God is going to rescue the momentary and seasonal losses of singleness, nor the overall big-picture loss that we may feel when we wake up one day and realize our story isn't turning out the way we thought it would. I don't know all His plans for improving the opportunities for His love and our lives from these unexpectedly single moments, days and years—and maybe even lifetimes. We may not fully understand the redemptive gain from our singleness this side of heaven, but I believe God has redemptive moments, seasons, and experiences for all of us.

Experiences like one thirty-something single woman had around a bonfire. She had thoroughly enjoyed a season of regular gatherings with friends, including brothers in Christ, at someone's house. The times together usually included a meal, sometimes a game. But the nights she loved most were the ones spent outside around a fire, laughing and talking.

When that season came to an end, it brought confusion, disappointment, and loss of male friendship. She began to ask the Lord to bring new brothers into her life. One evening a few years later, she sat around a bonfire with a new group of both sisters and brothers in Christ. She suddenly realized God had redeemed not only the loss of brotherly relationships, but also those fun experiences around a fire. God had given her not just a redemptive moment, but redemptive ongoing relationships in a redemptive season.

A single rose brought a redemptive moment for another unmarried woman. She has always desired to have children and has lived much of her life around them, both as a labor and delivery coach and a Christian school teacher.

"I love celebrating new babies," she says. "Watching most of my girlfriends get married and have babies has been hard at times. I snuggle those warm, sweet babies, and I'm genuinely glad for my friends. But, at the end of the day, there's no white, ruffled bassinet next to my bed. There's no husband doting on junior and no little cousins to add to the mix at holidays."

And for her, as is the case for many single and childless women, Mother's Day can sometimes prove challenging. So it was one year when all the mothers received roses at church that morning.

"I was sad that day because being single and childless was never a desire of mine," she says. "I was headed out to the car after the service, and one of the older gentlemen quickly followed after me. He handed me a rose and said, 'You need to know that you are a mother to many. God sees and your church sees all that you pour into our kids. Thank you for being one of our best moms.'"

The Lord replaced her feelings of loss with honor. He gave her the mother's gift, a rose of recognition signifying the spiritual children that filled her life.

These are the losses of singleness—friendship and motherhood, physical affection and companionship, masculine help and perspective—that God will redeem. These losses vary from woman to woman, from season to season. Yet, in a moment, or a season, God turns those losses into gains with His own presence and work. He shows us in special ways that He knows what we feel, and He turns it into an opportunity for us to receive something from Him: the embrace of a child, the appreciation of motherhood, the friendship of brothers around a fire on a cold night.

But beyond this, I believe God will bring many of us to a redemptive chapter in our lives that enables us to look back over years of singleness and waiting and wondering, and realize how God fulfilled His purpose in all of it.

I don't know how He will do it. I don't know what that will be like in your life, or in mine. But the question is, will we recognize it when it comes?

Elizabeth did. This older woman, the long-time barren mother of John the Baptist, was past hoping for a child. Over the years, Elizabeth and her husband, Zacharias, had prayed for a child (Luke 1:13). But by the time Luke picks up her story, her aging body had made conception impossible. It's doubtful she was expecting to be another Sarah, bearing another Isaac.

That is, until the day her husband came home mute in disbelief after an angel prophesied that they would have a son. And so Elizabeth conceived, responding to the miracle in joy and wonder. And, I believe, in recognition that God had been up to something greater all along. For here is what she said: "This is the way the Lord has dealt with me in the days when He looked with favor upon me, to take away my disgrace among men" (Luke 1:25, NAS).

My own translation: "So *this* is what God has been up to this whole time!" As if she had been waiting to see how the Lord would end her situation, respond to her years of prayer. Expecting some kind of purpose in her barrenness, some kind of fruitfulness from her life.

Expecting something—redemption, perhaps. And now a redemptive chapter began, bringing with it greater understanding and purpose, a purpose that prepared the way for the Messiah.

My pastor, Dale Evrist, says that when the "harvest" is later—later in life, and unexpectedly long in coming—it's greater. That's what Elizabeth experienced. And Hannah, and Sarah, and Joseph and Job. These all lived through seasons that required waiting and perseverance, stewardship and faith. Seasons that allowed them, like us, to sow more seeds of faith and faithfulness, unto a greater harvest.

In these seasons, the branch of the believer becomes more mature, able to bear greater fruit. As Pastor Dale says, "God knows how to redeem the time." He works deliberately, unhurried and purposefully, while the sown seeds grow.[21]

That kind of sowing, that kind of faith, is the way God wants us to respond to His sovereignty, to participate in the redemption He desires to bring.

NOTES

1. Kathy Troccoli, "A New Thing," KathyTroccoli.com (blog), accessed December 2012, http://www.kathytroccoli.com (blog post no longer available).

2. Ernest Becker, *The Denial of Death* (New York: Free Press, 1973), 160, 167, as quoted by Timothy Keller in *Counterfeit Gods* (New York: Dutton, 2009), 28.

3. James Strong, L.L.D., S.T.D., *Strong's Concordance*, BlueLetterBible.org, http://blueletterbible.org/lang/lexicon/lexicon.cfm?Strongs=G1805&t=KJV.

4. James Strong, L.L.D., S.T.D., *New Strong's Concise Dictionary of the Words in the Greek Testament* in *The New Strong's Exhaustive Concordance of the Bible* (Nashville: Thomas Nelson, 1995), 32.

5. Jason Gray, Notes on "Everything Sad is Coming Untrue" in *Everything Sad is Coming Untrue, Special Edition.* Centricity Music, 2009, compact disc.

6. Philip Yancey, *Disappointment with God* (Grand Rapids, MI: Zondervan, 1988), 72.

7. Robert Morgan, *The Promise* (Nashville: B & H Publishing Group, 2008), 171, 142.

8. Matthew Henry, *Matthew Henry's Commentary on the Whole Bible, Unabridged, Volume V, Matthew to John*, Luke 2, "Christ and Simeon in the Temple; Anna in the Temple," Christian Classics Ethereal Library, accessed November 17, 2009, http://www.ccel.org/ccel/henry/mhc5.Luke.iii.html.

9. Helen Gwilliam, "Anna," Ekklesia 4 Him, accessed November 17, 2009, http://www.ekklesia4him.net/anna.html.

10. Henry, *Matthew Henry's Commentary on the Whole Bible,* Luke 2, "Christ and Simeon in the Temple; Anna in the Temple."

11. Jack W. Hayford, Litt.D, Note on Ruth 1:8-9 in the *Spirit-Filled Life Bible*, ed. Jack W. Hayford, Litt.D (Nashville: Thomas Nelson, 1991), 1714.George A. Buttrick, ed.,

12. George A. Buttrick, ed., *The Interpreter's Dictionary of the Bible, Volume R-Z* (Nashville: Abingdon Press, 1962), 842.

13. Harold L. Willmington, *Willmington's Bible Handbook* (Wheaton: Tyndale House Publishers, 1997), 138.

14. Yitzchak Etshalom, "Analysis of Megillat Ruth (II)," Torah.org, 2005-2007, http://www.torah.org/advanced/mikra/5757/bm/Ruth2.html.

15. Yitzchak Etshalom, "Megillat Ruth (IV)," Torah.org, 2005-2007, http://torah.org/advanced/mikra/5757/bm/Ruth4.html.

16. "Harvest Seasons of Ancient Israel," Grace Communications International, accessed 2011. http://www.gci.org/law/festivals/harvest.

17. Yitzchak Etshalom, "Analysis of Megillat Ruth (V)," Torah.org, 2005-2007, http://www.torah.org/advanced/mikra/5757/bm/Ruth5.html#.

18. Ibid.

19. Marty McCall, "O Taste the Lord" (BMG Music/ASCAP, 1997) on *Images of Faith*, compact disc (Warner Bros. Records Inc., 1997).

20. Jason Gray and Randall Goodgame, "Everything Sad is Coming Untrue" on *Everything Sad is Coming Untrue, Special Edition,* compact disc (Franklin, TN: Centricity Music, 2009).

21. Dale Evrist, "Christmas Connections: Mary & Elizabeth" (sermon, New Song Christian Fellowship, Brentwood, TN, December 23, 2008).

"...WAY DOWN DEEP INSIDE OF ME IS A HOPE THAT SAYS, 'THIS CAN'T ALL BE FOR NOTHING. THERE HAS TO BE SOMETHING REDEEMABLE FROM THIS. THERE HAS TO BE A BIGGER PURPOSE THAN I KNOW OR CAN SEE.' "

- Denise Hildreth Jones[1]

– Chapter 6 –

Responding *to* Sovereignty

Her life, then, would not turn out as she expected, the kind of marriage she envisioned would never take place. Persian officials were at the door, ready to lead her to the palace. The king's beauty contest was in full swing, and beautiful young virgins were being sought from every province to participate.

And Esther was beautiful. She had not escaped notice. But her true nationality had. *Esther* was only her Persian name. Her birth name was as Hebrew as she was: *Hadassah*, the Hebrew word for the fragrant myrtle tree, deeply valued as a symbol of peace and prosperity, displayed during the Feast of Tabernacles.[2] She was aptly named, then—elegant and lovely like the fragrant tree, its white flowers striking against berry-laden evergreen branches. Perhaps her mother and father, who had never seen their homeland, chose a name that would help their daughter remember who she was: part of God's chosen people, loved, and preserved no matter where they lived.

For they lived in Persia, pagan and hostile, a place where their ancestors had originally been held as captives under the last king of Judah. In time the Persians conquered their captors, the Babylonians, and let the Israelites go home. But many of them remained where they had settled throughout Persia, having known no other home.[3] Hadassah's family was among them.

Yet, Esther was raised with a Jewish heritage in a Persian world, thanks to her devout uncle Mordecai—Mordecai, who would not bow down and worship a heathen palace official. Prudent and patriotic Mordecai, whose recorded words and actions speak of a reverent faith in God and awareness of His sovereign work. Faithful Mordecai, who reared the orphan child Hadassah, who advised the young woman Esther.

And so, more than likely, Hadassah dreamed Jewish dreams in an anti-Semitic world. Marriage to a Hebrew man with faith in her God, perhaps. Marriage to a man, at least, with the same character and values as Mordecai. She would have dreamed of having children, so important for a woman of that time. Surely, with an advocate as righteous and respected as Mordecai, finding a suitable husband would have been possible.

But the king's decree changed all that. Perhaps most of the other virgins in the region trembled with excitement: a chance to become royalty, the prospect of living in a palace with servants, riches, and recognition. A woman could not find a better position or better security.

But Esther may have wanted more than security. Esther might have thought about it through Hebrew values. Marriage to an ungodly king? Xerxes, a man so different from Mordecai—a man who could be harsh or kind on a whim, a man who must be feared and obeyed? Everyone knew how he dismissed former Queen Vashti when she refused to prance herself before the self-indulgent king and his male guests. If Esther won the contest and became the new queen, would she be truly known and loved by her husband? Would she be part of a household that honored God?

If Esther did not become queen, she would remain part of the king's gigantic harem, never to become the wife of a God-fearing man—or anyone else, for that matter—with no guarantee that she would have the opportunity to become a mother.

But the officials had arrived, and Esther stepped across the threshold of her home. As she did, she left behind previous ideas about how her life might turn out.

NOT WHAT I EXPECTED

What Christian girl didn't grow up loving the story of Esther? Her life epitomizes the epic glory and adventure of history's maidens and literature's protagonists. She's the perfect beauty who wins the pageant, the courageous heroine who saves a nation. The underdog who marries the king, the queen who fulfills her legendary destiny.

She's the princess in what appears to be a biblical fairytale. But it is no fairytale. And as romantic or beautiful or significant as her story may seem, it required Esther to take the risk of trusting God with her life and her heart. She could not have played so important a role in history, fulfilled so great a divinely-orchestrated destiny, if she did not first entrust herself to Him.

We don't truly know Esther's expectations for her life before she came into that destiny. Yet, we can be sure she had expectations. And it's safe to assume they didn't include life in King Xerxes' palace.

Our stories may have more in common with Esther's than we thought. Like her, our dreams for marriage and motherhood are turning out differently than we expected. One friend experienced what probably exemplifies the most idealized picture of what many of us expected.

"Growing up, my mother always told me, 'You'll have a house and a husband and kids, and you'll live nearby and we'll be able to garden together and drink coffee in the morning while your babies nap.' So, I grew up with that expectation. My mom gave that expectation because that's all she knew, all her mother had known. But," she so rightly concludes, "we are a different generation."

My friend's mother is now in ill health, her father already in his seventies. None of her parents' three forty-something children are married, and there are no grandchildren. Not only did my friend's expectations not come to pass, neither did her mother's.

As many of us wonder if we will ever be wives and mothers, many of our parents wonder if they will ever be grandparents. Their disappointment is as real—and as unexpected—as ours.

What are we supposed to do when things don't work out the way we expected, especially if it's a way that seemed like it fit into God's overall plan for His people? Approaching forty made my reality sink in: I will never have a marriage and family during the prime of my childbearing years, as I always thought I would. That dream shattered over my milestone birthday, the sharp pieces pricking at my heart for many months afterward.

But Esther's response to God's sovereignty in the face of her unmet expectations inspires hope, and even anticipation. Whatever her expectations were, she had to let them go because something different was unfolding before her. And if God was sovereign over her life, then He had a purpose in letting circumstances created by an ungodly society redirect her life. Esther had to release her own expectations about her life before she could fulfill God's purpose for allowing her to be so beautiful, to be swept into the king's contest, to be the winner of Vashti's crown.

The God who designed us for marriage and motherhood is sovereign over every circumstance, including all those causing prolonged singleness. Marriage may not be unfolding for us in this season of life, but *something* is. His hand guides us as we travel the unexpected path, as it guided Esther.

The Bible doesn't talk about Esther's heart or emotions, her process of letting go, whether she needed a turning point. It doesn't talk explicitly about her faith. But it's there between the lines, enabling her to become a woman of wisdom, of inner radiance and outward composure—to be designated by an ungodly world as the best there was to offer a king. Faith is there in her trust of godly Mordecai, her heeding of his wise counsel to keep her nationality a secret as she goes to the palace. It's there when she calls her maidens to fast for her before she approaches the king uninvited. It's there in her courage to risk her life for the sake of her nation.

Ultimately, faith was Esther's response to God's sovereignty. Trust enabled her to see past her own plans and ideas for her life so she could participate in what God was taking her through in the present moment and see where it was going to lead.

And faith must have enabled her to believe that whatever different path God had placed her on, it was going to be worth it. It was going to be redemptive.

LIVING IN THE PRESENT MOMENT

She is a Christian counselor, and she is single. Quite a bit older, in fact, than the thirty-something woman who sits across from her today.

"How do you do it?" her unmarried client asks. "How do you handle continuing singleness?"

The counselor opens a file drawer filled with folders.

"These are all my dreams," she says, pointing toward the folders. Each folder is marked with something that represents a dream or desire of her heart.

"And this is what I focus on."

She pulls out a folder labeled *Today*.

Remember Lisa, whose turning point in chapter four came after she got tired of the blues? After her hope-filled encounter with the Lord, she determined to enjoy her life and prepare for marriage. She recalled one older single woman who would think, *Oh brother* whenever the pastor talked about marriage.

"When I was single, I would listen," Lisa said. "I wanted to learn." She would make a mental note and consider the words of the speaker rather than tune them out because they might make her feel sad or left out. To disregard teaching on marriage, she said, is to miss opportunities to prepare for it.

A woman with the *oh brother* mindset is still holding on to her own expectations about *what should have happened* in her life, a knot of disappointment still binding her heart. It is only when she lets go of what isn't that she can take hold of what *is*. What is true and good and happening right now, today. Because *today* is where we experience the abundant life of Christ.

It's not in the past when we were younger and, perhaps, thinner or less wrinkled. It's not in the daydreams about the future and the marriage it might hold. It's not in the fantasy of what our lives didn't turn out to be. It's in the present moment.

It's in the *right now* of life that we experience God's presence, that God does His work in and through us. It's in this moment that the Holy Spirit speaks to us and brings revelation. It's in this moment that we sit face-to-face with another person, encounter a situation, apprehend how God wants us to respond, or to give, or to pray.[4]

Living in the present moment doesn't mean we stop dreaming or desiring, stop praying or hoping for all that God has for us—for marriage, for motherhood, for ministry, for full provision. Not at all. All those file folders are still in the drawer, intact.

Nor does it mean we will never feel the pain of disappointment again. Instead, it means that by faith we release the life that hasn't happened into the safekeeping of God, trusting He will respond to our act of faith with absolute goodness—that "proving the good and acceptable will of God" kind of goodness Paul talks about in Romans 12:2. It is choosing to live face-forward and faith-filled in the reality of life today, acknowledging its purpose and value under God's sovereignty.

Like Esther, we have to let go of the life we expected to open ourselves to a new and different story. Otherwise, we'll miss the present moment and the abundance available in it. We can't move forward in the life He wants to give us if our heart is stuck in the non-reality of the life we haven't experienced. In that nebulous place, faith is not the primary operative, God's goodness not the primary focus, hope not the primary result.

A LIFETIME OF TODAYS

She is just past sixty years old. Deep in her heart she has always desired marriage. And she desires it still. In the meantime, though, she has things to do. People who need her listening ear. A ministry to help run. Healing and recovery groups to facilitate.

She's a merciful person who is aware and watchful of what's going on around her, of the people God allows to cross her path. In the many passing-by moments of her life, she stops to listen to someone pour out her story of sadness or pain, which happens everywhere she goes. No matter where she is, she listens and responds, bringing a fresh measure of God's grace and encouragement to the other person. Her life is a rich exhibit of redemptive fruit.

To me, this woman is an example of what it means to live in the present moment. She doesn't miss what God is doing around her and how He might use her *today*. As a result, she blesses so many people. Yes, she's honest about the disappointment of unmet expectations, about her journey of finding peace through her ongoing singleness, but she's always expressing her thankfulness for God's goodness in her life, enjoying the things He's given her. She works daily with close, life-long friends. She enjoys a special redemptive "auntie" relationship with the little boy she takes to church, and she played a part in leading his mother to Christ.

Life hasn't turned out the way this woman expected it to. But it has turned out to be good. It is a life built of *todays* lived in fulfillment of God's purposes.

If we've needed and gone through a turning point with our disappointment, then we're already better equipped to live in the present moment. If we have not taken our unfulfilled expectations to the Lord at all, then that's the first place to start.

Once we take our emotions about the past or the present to the Lord, then we are free to focus on *today*. But sometimes thoughts or emotions still break in, threatening to steal joy and hope. How do you stay on track for today? For me, there's one key above all others. And that is, simply, pursuing Jesus. Cultivating a close relationship with Him, every day.

JUST A CLOSER WALK WITH THEE

It is November of my fortieth year, and I'm on an overnight road trip to Chattanooga with a couple of single girlfriends. One of them is turning forty, and we are celebrating with a little get-away to a bed and breakfast wedged into a curve of a forest-lined road wrapped around Lookout Mountain. I sit alone in the back seat, marveling at the radiant autumn leaves, at the same time thinking about a special (male) friendship that recently ended. I feel a bit gloomy.

My friend in the front seat has just changed the music, and I tune in. It's the music of gospel worship artist Israel Houghton, and the words of his song reach into my soul:

Accepted, highly favored of the Lord
Forgiven, by Your love I am transformed…
Established, ever blameless in Your Son
Forever I am chosen to be loved…
I receive Your love, I receive Your love for me…[5]

I need this song, I think. *I need this whole album.* Every song that comes on celebrates the truth of who we are, who *I* am, in Christ—saved by grace, never forsaken, deeply loved, chosen.

This music reminds me of something I've been more intentional about—speaking the truth of God's Word about who I am and who He is over my life each day. I pray it. I declare it. I thank God for it. And with the right playlist, I can sing it.

Two months later, it is wintertime. I bundle up in a thickly lined, puffy brown suede coat that I can't part with because my mom bought it—and later re-stitched its shoulder seam—for me years ago. It is the perfect coat for my freezing cold walks with Jesus. Walks that I have recently reinstated as a regular—and hopefully daily—habit.

I plug in my ear buds and pop on my flashlight, stepping into the frosty pre-dawn darkness. As I look up at the moon cradling a newborn day, the first joyful beats of Israel Houghton's *Power of One* begin. And my heart comes alive.

Worship music and personal worship time has been a part of my daily life for years. But during my turning point season, it became a renewed strategy. I intentionally sought out songs that proclaimed doctrinal truths about God and my position in Christ. I created a playlist on my phone with songs about the death and resurrection of Christ, what He accomplished for me, and worshipful responses to Him.

Keeping the cross before me, reminding myself how great Jesus is, how lovingly and kindly and mercifully He thinks of me, keeps me living in the present moment *with Him*. It has restored a measure of joy to my days.

On my walks with Jesus, I usually listen to songs from my special playlist on the way out, then pray on the way back. The songs have become part of my meditation. They, along with the Scriptures I read, flow back into my mind and over my heart throughout the day. In present-tense. At any given moment.

No matter where I am or what I'm doing, the words of God are always true. And in this way, I receive God's love and grace in my life. Not just the mental acknowledgement of them, but the actual experience of them. And that experience, that reality of His love and presence, is what I desperately need. It is this kind of communion with Jesus throughout the day that keeps me steady and engaged in the moment.

A NIGHT ABOUT JESUS

It was Valentine's Day, another one. And they were all still single.

It would have been easy to miss the present moment when the holiday for lovebirds only stirs up disappointment about what hasn't happened in the past or longing for what might happen in the future. It would have been easy to dwell in *oh brother*. But a particular group of single women didn't miss out on the abundant life God had for them that day. In their own creative way, they turned their hearts toward Jesus, seeking to woo *Him*. One of them described the evening:

> We hosted an elegant dinner party in His honor. Delicious food, over one hundred candles in the living room and dining room, and roses on the table. We had each come with love letters to the Lord to tuck under our plates. After dinner, we moved to the living room for praise and worship by candlelight. It was so refreshing, so filling, and we could just sense the Lord's pleasure.

These women enjoyed an evening of friendship with one another and a deepening relationship with Jesus. They celebrated Him in a special, beautiful setting. They took a night that might normally have them focusing on themselves and their own unfulfilled desires and turned it into a night about Him. They loved Him and received His love, which is really the essence of cultivating an intimate relationship with Him.

They turned it into a night about Him. Isn't everything ultimately supposed to be about Him? Isn't that how we respond to His sovereign Lordship over our lives? Living in the present moment—it is about us enjoying our lives with Him, living our lives for Him, telling others about Him. Letting His life flow from us to others. It's what Jesus called abiding in Him, the way a branch is intricately connected to the vine. And it only happens moment by moment, when we are tuned in to Him and to what's happening around us.

WHAT HANGS IN THE BALANCE

She has a decision to make, and her stomach churns.

Uncle Mordecai had sent the document she holds in her trembling hand, a copy of the awful death decree issued to every Persian province. The Jews must be killed. Haman, the official her uncle refused to bow before, is behind the law. His motive is to take revenge upon Mordecai by annihilating his entire race.

What Haman and the king don't know is that she, the queen, is part of that race. And now, at least in Mordecai's view, it's that very queen who alone is in a position to do something about the death sentence. Along with the decree, he had sent this message: *Go in to the king and plead before him for your people.*

Didn't he know it is against the law to approach the king in his court without being asked? Esther hadn't been summoned all month. Didn't Uncle Mordecai know the penalty for breaking the law would be death? Unless, of course, the king was in a good mood and held out his golden scepter at the interruption. But who could guarantee he would do that?

Esther's decision is not easy. If she does nothing—takes the passive path of self-preservation—her people will die. If she steps out in faith, *she* could die. Esther has to let Mordecai know her life is at stake.

In response, Mordecai delivers his now-famous statement with a perspective that reveals his insight into God's sovereignty:

> Do not think in your heart that you will escape in the king's palace any more than all the other Jews. For if you remain

> completely silent at this time, relief and deliverance will arise for the Jews from another place, but you and your father's house will perish. Yet who knows whether you have come to the kingdom for such a time as this? (Esther 4:13-14, NKJV)

Esther thinks about his words, and makes her decision. She would do it.

As believers, we like to quote Mordecai's "such a time as this" phrase to encourage each other about our calling in different seasons or situations. But Mordecai was communicating more than encouragement to Esther. He turned the idea of God's sovereign purpose into a matter of her responsibility. Mordecai's focus is not that Esther could lose her life if she goes before the king, but that she will surely lose her life if she does not. He knows God's purpose for the nation will be fulfilled, but God's purpose for Esther as an individual could be thwarted by her own decision. Mordecai's statement is a warning that Esther not miss the purpose for which God had made her queen.

It's a weighty subject to think about. Not just for Esther, but for us. What does it matter if we fail to engage in the reality of the present moment? Esther's story shows us it does matter. Somehow, in some way, our circumstances—unwanted or not—do matter. If Esther had chickened out and never approached King Xerxes, she would have died without fulfilling God's purpose for her life, the very reason His sovereignty allowed her circumstances to be what they were.

What hangs in the balance, ultimately, is our experiencing the fulfillment of God's purpose in our singleness, of His plan for our lives. His unexpected plan, the one we never thought of and the one that affects other people, too. The one as significant and epic as Esther's. The one in which He predestined to showcase His grace and work in our lives, and to the world. Because He has that kind of plan for all of us, whether it encompasses marriage or not.

Esther engaged in her circumstances and prepared to step out in faith. She asked the Jews in the city to pray and fast for her, then boldly stood in the court where King Xerxes could see her.

I bet she was trembling, her heart pounding harder and harder as he turned his head, caught her eye. Breathing a deep, shaky sigh as he lifted the golden scepter and extended it toward her. And then a flood of light, insight, realization. Maybe even like that of Elizabeth's when she found out she was pregnant.

So this is what God has been up to all this time!

That was only the first step. Esther initiated a set of banquets during which she finally made her nationality known. The king, angry with Haman, executed him immediately. Then Esther dared to once again go before the king uninvited, asking him to make a decree empowering the Jews to fight back.

In the end, Esther's intervention, through God's sovereignty, saved her people. And God's sovereignty saved her. All along, before Haman concocted his plan, before Vashti was even dismissed from the palace, God was moving to position one of His own—a young woman—to bring deliverance to the people He loved. And when the day came that the Jews needed an advocate, Esther was already there for God to work through.

Esther's unexpected life became the redemptive circumstance that rescued a nation from death. The account in the Bible ends not only with the glory that a nation is saved; it ends with Esther's personal joy of having Mordecai appointed to the palace in Haman's place, in one sense reuniting her with him there. Perhaps she had feared leaving him, her only family, behind when she went to the palace as a virgin. If so, then even in that personal desire of her heart, God provided in an unexpected—and incredibly redemptive—way.

Like Esther, we have a choice to make. It is whether we will risk our lives—and our hearts—by releasing our unfulfilled dreams to Him and engaging in the life we never expected.

"We have to take that risk if we're going to live the kind of lives God has called us to live, to be the people God dreamed of when He thought us into existence," writes pastor and author Pete Wilson. "So many miss out on this designed life because we make an unconscious vow that we will only trust ourselves and the things we think we can control."[6]

OF EPIC PROPORTIONS

She was a woman, and a princess, but she had a passion to fight, to do something great and noteworthy. When the men rode out to war, she disguised herself as a soldier and rode with them.

Her name is Eowyn. She's one of the beautiful heroines in J. R. R. Tolkien's *The Lord of the Rings* trilogy, which is a tale of epic proportions—of hobbits and dwarfs, of elves and men, even the occasional princess here and there—coming together to save Middle Earth from destruction. The story is wonderful, fantastical, and adventurous. Glorious, as the courage and choices of individuals contribute to the overall triumph of good over evil. I love stories like that.

In the final book, *The Return of the King*, Eowyn plays her part. In the middle of a battle with not-so-great-odds for winning, she defies the deadliest representative of the enemy: the Lord of the Nazgul, an evil, armor-clad spirit with unmatched power. As Eowyn steps between him and her injured uncle, the king, he threatens to capture and torture her. The narrative describes her response:

> "Do what you will; but I will hinder it, if I may."
> "Hinder me? Thou fool. No living man may hinder me!"
> …the clear voice was like the ring of steel. "But no living man am I! You look upon a woman. Eowyn I am, Eomund's daughter. You stand between me and my lord and kin. Begone, if you be not deathless! For living or dark undead, I will smite you, if you touch him."[7]

With her sword, Eowyn courageously cuts off the head of the lord's winged dragon, and he lunges in anger toward her. With a swing of his imposing mace, he shatters her shield and breaks her arm. Eowyn falls to her knees in pain. The lord raises his mace above her when one of the hobbits stabs the lord's leg, causing him to miss. Eowyn seizes the moment.

> Then tottering, struggling up, with her last strength she drove her sword between crown and mantle, as the great shoulders bowed before her. The sword broke sparkling into many shards.

> The crown rolled away with a clang. Eowyn fell forward upon her fallen foe. But lo! the mantle and hauberk were empty. Shapeless they lay now on the ground, torn and tumbled; and a cry went up into the shuddering air, and faded to a shrill wailing, passing with the wind, a voice bodiless and thin that died, and was swallowed up and was never heard again in that age of the world.[8]

The Lord of the Nazgul had correctly boasted that he could not be hindered by a mere man, because a prophecy proclaimed such about him long ages before. It turned out that only a woman could do the job.

Sometimes, when I read the book of Revelation, the visions of Daniel and Ezekiel, or the stories of Elijah and Elisha, I feel like I'm reading a fantasy tale like *The Lord of the Rings*. When I consider the idea of God coming to earth in human form, dying to save His people, then triumphantly rising from the tomb, it seems fantastical and fictitious like a movie, too incredibly good to be true.

But it is true. And people like Tolkien have the ability to dream up stories of epic proportions because they are already part of such a story themselves. One that God created and is not yet finished. He redeemed you and me as individuals to play a significant part in it.

I'll be the first to admit that my role never feels heroic. I'm not Eowyn or Esther. I'm not even Hannah or Ruth or Elizabeth.

But often, I feel something inside me that identifies with the passionate prayers of these biblical women, with the desire of the fictional character Eowyn. Her great fear was to live as if in a cage, "to stay behind bars, until use and old age accept them, and all chance of doing great deeds is gone beyond recall or desire."[9]

I think that's at the heart of our dreams and desires—to fulfill a greater purpose than what our lives sometimes appear to have. In a word, as daughters of the one true King, we desire to be *fruitful.* Desires for marriage and motherhood are a natural part of that. Sometimes it feels like the strength, fullness, and opportunities they might bring, especially in the realm of partnership, are in danger of passing "beyond recall or desire."

The unmet expectations of our lives need not and must not be a cage that holds us back from doing Eowyn's "great deeds" in the kingdom. We don't have to wait for marriage for our lives to get started, to flourish, to be fruitful. Our lives and stories matter *today*. One forty-something woman says she doesn't want to get to heaven and say, "'God, I didn't do anything because You didn't bring me a husband.'

"There's always a choice to resent that things haven't happened the way we wanted them to, or to simply endure them. The Lord showed me how to joyfully embrace them," she says. "For me, it's all about not living life in limbo, but for kingdom purposes. When we tap into God's ultimate purpose about doing kingdom work, it helps in not feeling so desperate for marriage. If nothing else, I want to get to heaven and have God say, 'well done' and to have been fruitful, not having been married. I can bear living without a husband, but I can't bear not being fruitful."

Not living life in limbo. Fruitfulness is produced in the opposite place of *limbo,* in present-moment living, even when those moments feel long, insignificant, or disappointing. Women like Ruth, Hannah, and Anna lived seemingly unremarkable lives that contained not-meant-to-be circumstances before their stories reached a redemptive zenith of more obvious destiny-fulfillment. Each of them had to remain faithful to God and engaged in His momentary purposes day by day, season by season, before they experienced or even understood their full destinies.

The challenge is to believe, and keep believing, that God has something He wants to do in the present season, even when it doesn't look like life is moving toward the destination we desire. One writer, Alicia Britt Chole, calls these kinds of seasons, in which we feel hidden, the anonymous years. Sometimes, prolonged singleness makes me feel hidden, like a random lady in the audience, not the princess chosen for a grand destiny.

But faithfulness to God in these "anonymous" seasons is what develops fruit and brings about the destiny He has planned. Chole writes about the way Jesus lived faithfully in obedience to and intimacy with the Father during the hidden years of His life before he was released into public ministry, before He could complete His purpose for coming to Earth.

> As it was with his Son, so it is with us: being hidden by God's hand is a good and perfect gift… Though unapplauded, our anonymous seasons are not even remotely unproductive. In them, God cultivates strengths that stand the test of time… Such strengths are not *given*; they are *grown*. They are the fruit

> of active participation, not passive observation. Anonymous seasons can be the most spiritually fruitful spaces of our lives if we respect their potential and cooperate with God in their development.[10]

When our todays are lived in God's unfolding purpose, they grow into a life of epic proportions.

REACHING FOR REDEMPTION

What dreams do the lovely daughters of God dream in a faithless world? Like Esther, our God-centered dreams and expectations clash against the society in which we live. And like her, that is the very reason we have been placed here. Our lives as believers are destined for the unexpected from the very beginning. Esther discovered God had more for her than the typical Jewish dream.

What if God has more for us than the typical American dream, even the Christian version? More than the white picket fence, the house, the husband, two cars and two kids?

That's not to say our lives won't be blessed and good. That's not even to say we will never get married, that marriage and children aren't a part of His plan or our destiny. But what He has for us goes far beyond our dreams.

I heard a pastor say that when we open our hands in surrender to the Lord, we have to expect that He's going to fill them with something, something we have to take hold of in faith. In Philippians, Paul identifies what that is:

> Not that I have already obtained it or have already become perfect, but I press on so that I may lay hold of that for which also I was laid hold of by Christ Jesus. Brethren, I do not regard myself as having laid hold of it yet; but one thing I do: forgetting what lies behind and reaching forward to what lies ahead, I press on toward the goal for the prize of the upward call of God in Christ Jesus. (Philippians 3:12-14, NAS)

Paul calls it the "upward call of God." It's the more-than-the-American-dream that God has for us, the more-than-the-Jewish-dream that Esther experienced. It's God's dream.

The Greek word Paul uses for *upward* is *ano*, meaning "above, on high; of the quarters of the heaven, northward; of countries, inland, up from the coast."[11] It describes a call, then, that reaches far beyond our country, city, street—or picket fence. It's a call that has to do with more than our current life.

The word he uses for call, *klesis*, has this definition: "a call, invitation—to a feast or of the divine invitation to embrace salvation of God." It's the shorter form of the word *kaleo*, which means "to call aloud, to invite, to call by name or to give a name to."[12]

The upward call is personal and specific to you, to me. Yet, it is eternal at the same time. It encompasses all of humanity and the forever that we can't comprehend, and it is close enough to include our individual names.

Taking hold of the upward call of God is accepting the invitation to play a personal role in God's eternal plan for humankind. That may not sound very specific, but that's because the details can only be worked out in the circumstances of an individual's life at a certain point in history, as we see in Esther's story.

We can do it, because Jesus did it first—to redeem us. He let go of all that should have been His to take hold of all that should have been ours (Hebrews 12:2). His upward call was to lower Himself and become human. Only then could He redeem us, because only a human could pay the price for sin. He laid hold of obedience, redeeming the first human man's disobedience. He took the risk Adam and Eve didn't—trusting the Father fully and completely in all things.

And so, He let go. Let go of His equality with God—Paul said He did not regard it as something to be grasped, something to hold on to. He let go of His right to be King, of all that was meant to be for the Son of God.

He laid hold of humility, wrapping Himself in human flesh. He took hold of our sin and sickness, bore in His body the reality of our shame. He took hold of the cross. He took hold of death. Then He let that go, reaching for resurrection.

When we take hold of the upward call in Him, we reach for redemption.

NOTES

1. Denise Hildreth Jones, *Flying Solo* (Ventura, CA: Regal Books, 2010), 86.

2. J.D. Douglas and Merrill C. Tenney, *New International Bible Dictionary* (Grand Rapids, Michigan: Zondervan, 1987), 802.

3. Herbert Lockyer, Sr., ed., *Illustrated Dictionary of the Bible* (Nashville: Thomas Nelson Publishers, 1986), 355-57.

4. Farrar Moore with Sheryl Cook and Betty Plank, *From Hurt to Hope* (Nashville: Caring Resources, 2007), 19-20.

5. Israel Houghton and Peter Wilson, "I Receive" on *Power of One*, compact disc (Integrity/Columbia, 2009).

6. Pete Wilson, *Plan B* (Nashville: Thomas Nelson, 2009), 44.

7. J. R. R. Tolkien, *The Return of the King* (New York, NY: Ballantine Books, 1983), 127.

8. Ibid., 128-129.

9. Ibid., 62.

10. Alicia Britt Chole, *anonymous* (Nashville: Integrity Publishers, 2006), 169-170.

11. James Strong, L.L.D., S.T.D., *New Strong's Concise Dictionary of the Words in the Greek Testament* in *The New Strong's Exhaustive Concordance of the Bible* (Nashville: Thomas Nelson, 1995), 9.

12. Ibid., 50.

"This way is for the brave. It ignores the values culture has pressed into its hand... It allows God to be God. It expects Him to move, but not to fit."

- Margaret Becker[1]

– Chapter 7 –
Counting Loss as Gain

It is late summer, and I have been forty for a few months. I am at the beginning of my turning point season, meeting with my counselor, grasping rays of light that reach to a darkness I don't dare mention to many people. I feel vulnerable, but I don't necessarily want it to show.

One Saturday I get out all my pretty tea things to set my table-for-two by the sunny kitchen window, place in its center colorful zinnias my sister planted for me on my birthday, and fill the yellow kettle with water. I choose the pearl-enameled teapot and the vintage cream and yellow teacups with sketches of simple brown leaves.

We drink tea for hours that day, my tea-loving friend and I. We both relish the lingering, the sipping of a strong, dark cup with a spot of milk. We savor my homemade bread with butter, her homemade scones with jam. We welcome the brewing of another pot.

Our conversation is pleasant and meaningful. Eventually the talk turns toward our unexpected stories, continuing singleness and its disappointments. And then I see tears in her eyes.

She's working toward a turning point of her own. I feel her loss, and I feel mine. This could be a sadness that we brush away, stuff back into the closet. I could wait with my eyes cast down while she blinks the tears back into her own hidden reservoir of pain. Or I could turn our tea party into a pity party, push empathy toward despondence, unravel our spirits down to flesh.

But thoughts have appeared at the front of my mind, thoughts about what I've been learning through my own feelings of loss. It is my personal story, and I want to keep it private. I could ignore that prompting toward vulnerability.

Instead, I decide to tell her some details about my valley of disappointment that I have told very few, some things I discovered hidden in my emotional closet. I tell her because I want to share the rays of light I've been given.

We talk. She dares to tell me more of her details, and then we pray. And afterwards we both feel better, more hopeful. In the following days, she tells me about some of her own breakthrough moments, her own light rays that came in answer to our prayers.

My story really does matter, even the parts about disappointment. My willingness to share it created a redemptive moment for her, one that Jesus could use for His work in her life. One He could use to fulfill His purpose in mine.

REDEEMING THE TIME

My little tea party incident might seem insignificant. But it wasn't. It was a present-moment thing, a doorway where the abundant life of Jesus could enter. I think it's one small example of what Paul was talking about in Ephesians 5:15-17: "See then that you walk circumspectly, not as fools but as wise, redeeming the time, because the days are evil. Therefore do not be unwise, but understand what the will of the Lord is" (NKJV).

Circumspectly—what a fabulous word. A simpler translation of it in other Bible versions is *carefully*. Taking hold of the upward call in the present moment means we take care to notice our surroundings, the lives of others, and the voice of the Spirit. We understand this is the Lord's will—to walk as the children of light that we already are in Him, as described in the preceding verses of Ephesians 5.

Children of light, even in our seasons of darkness. Because we have Jesus, we always have means to redeem the time, to make the most of every opportunity, as some translations say. We rescue moments from loss, from unwise waste, by seeking the gain of Christ and His abundant life in each of them. In the words of pastor and writer Robert Morgan, "Over and over, if we train ourselves to see it, our worst problems become our best pulpits... He takes our bad news and turns it into opportunities for sharing His Good News."[2]

That's why present-moment living is so important—it's not just about us receiving the abundant life we desperately need. It's about us receiving so we have something to give away. It is the giving—the listening, the serving, the speaking of mercy and truth—that redeems the time with kingdom purposes. As we look for the redemption of our own losses, we must allow God to make us part of the redemptive moments, relationships, and seasons He has for others.

And that's why our stories matter, even the disappointing parts. Embedded in those disappointments are the seeds of redemption not only for ourselves, but for others. As we wait for God to redeem our losses, He can bring gain from them to someone else. Farrar Moore and Sheryl Cook say it this way: "I must remember that it's *never* all about me. God would never be so inefficient as to make anything just all about me. He will *always* use my circumstances to accomplish His purposes in and for others, too."[3]

Redeeming the time may not always mean spilling your heart to another person, as I did over tea. The Holy Spirit puts us in the lives of different people for various reasons, and He wants to use our voice, story, gifts and personality in ways that are fitting and unique for each situation. But God's call to redeem the time most definitely means that our singleness—yours, mine, and ours as an older generation of women—has a part to play in the process.

Our singleness matters. And it's not all about us.

THE LOSS THAT MATTERED

She was single again. *Widow.* A harsh word, a sad word. A word that created challenges for her in this new land where she lived with her mother-in-law.

She was a poor woman, and she did a poor woman's work. She spent each day outdoors in the fields, gathering the crops left behind by the harvesters. And with the food she gathered, she supported both herself and her mother-in-law.

And so, day after day, Ruth gleaned.

Ruth gleaned.

I like to think of Ruth's gleaning as a symbolic picture of living in the present moment. No doubt she still went through times of pain and frustration. But Ruth faithfully lived the life in front of her. She redeemed the time by serving God and serving Naomi as well. Her presence was God's mercy and goodness in Naomi's life.

And her singleness mattered. Because of it, Ruth could take advantage of the law that commanded reapers to leave grain and grapes during harvest for widows to gather (Deut. 24:19-21). Through this circumstance, Ruth received God's provision and discovered His heart of compassion for widows. Even though their position was lowly, widows were under the "special care of God who provides [them] with food and clothing" (Deut. 10:18).[4]

And because of Ruth's singleness, her label *widow*, she was an eligible participant in the law of levirate marriage on Naomi's behalf. Her singleness became the thing that redeemed Naomi's singleness, through her levirate marriage to Boaz.

But who's to say her singleness didn't redeem Boaz's?

Read between the lines in the book of Ruth, and you will see that a compelling love story, and not just a legal transaction, transpires. In the Old Testament, marriages were arranged, and "falling in love" did not necessarily factor into the equation. In levirate marriage, widows were given or promised to other men in the family only to bear offspring for the deceased.5 I think it's significant that Boaz, and not the other eligible kinsman redeemer, married Ruth. Significant because he loved her.

Boaz, the God-fearing land owner, did more than obey the law in his treatment of widows—at least, for this particular widow. He told Ruth not to go to another field, but to stay in his for the entire harvest season. He commanded his reapers not to touch her and to leave behind extra wheat and barley specifically for her to collect. He invited her, a foreign woman, to eat and drink with himself and the other reapers.

Boaz had noticed her, and Ruth was mystified. "Why have I found favor in your eyes, that you should take notice of me, since I am a foreigner?" (Ruth 2:10, NKJV). Boaz responded:

> It has been fully reported to me, all that you have done for your mother-in-law since the death of your husband, and how you have left your father and your mother and the land of your birth, and have come to a people whom you did not know before. The Lord repay your work, and a full reward be given you by the Lord God of Israel, under whose wings you have come for refuge. (Ruth 2:11-12, NKJV)

Boaz had heard about Ruth's character and kindness, and he was impressed. Now, here she was in person, working in his field. He did what any man of good character with some level of interest in a woman would do. He took care of her.

The scholar Rabbi Etshalom implies Boaz was interested in Ruth, writing that he "favored her in ways that indicated a special affection."[6] Boaz cared about Ruth personally, extending to her more than the general concern for welfare that he might have shown to other gleaners.

Why then, assuming he was aware of his position as a potential kinsman redeemer, didn't he pursue her? Notes in my Bible propose "that due to his age he may have been shy in approaching her, which necessitated Ruth's approaching him."[7] Maybe he was waiting for the other kinsman to act first, or maybe he really didn't think he had a chance.

But he did. And who knows what special redemptive blessing Ruth could have been in his life? Could he have experienced some loss of his own that left him thinking he would not end up with a woman like her?

When Ruth approached him at the threshing floor as Naomi said, Boaz saw it as a great kindness that she came to him rather than to younger men. Notes in my Bible state, "Boaz's words seem to suggest that young men were attracted to Ruth."[8] His wasn't the only head that Ruth had turned, nor was his the youngest. She was somewhat of a novelty, as the people in town were well aware of Naomi's return with her exceptionally kind daughter-in-law. Perhaps people were watching to see where she would end up, following her unfolding story.

So when their betrothal became public at the city gate, everyone who heard about it cheered. The people and town elders did not merely approve of the marriage as a duty, they rejoiced in God's blessing and favor over *Boaz*. Their words create a picture of curious onlookers who knew Ruth's story and, most certainly, knew Boaz's story as well. They sang:

"May the Lord make the woman who is coming into your home like Rachel and Leah, both of whom built the house of Israel; and may you achieve wealth in Ephrathah and become famous in Bethlehem. Moreover, may your house be like the house of Perez whom Tamar bore to Judah, through the offspring which the Lord will give you by this young woman" (Ruth 4:11-12, NKJV).

Whatever wealth and love and family Boaz may have already had, God multiplied it by bringing Ruth into his life. She, the widowed foreigner, brought renown to *him*, an already successful and respected man.

The Scripture doesn't reveal any loss or hardship Boaz may have faced in his past, but I wouldn't be surprised if this love, later in his life, had special meaning for him.

Ruth redeemed the time through her faithfulness to God, both in her day-to-day life with Naomi and later in her availability and willingness to marry Boaz. Ruth was one of those people who brought kindness, service, and gain to other people wherever she went. All this, through her own loss.

When we live faith-first in all situations, that's what Jesus does with our personalities, our stories, and even our singleness.

CARRYING REDEMPTION'S COST

It is still wintertime, and I am, Lord willing, nearing the end of my turning point season. Letting go of disappointment. Seeing my story in a new way, taking hold of God's purpose. Keeping the cross before me.

And so, the words of the Apostle Paul cut to the heart. "But I want you to know, brethren, that the things which happened to me have actually turned out for the furtherance of the gospel," he says in Philippians 1:12.

What things? Oh, things like imprisonment—"my chains," as Paul says. And we know that many other things happened to him, too—beatings, shipwrecks, hunger, injustice. But Paul viewed all these losses as gains for the gospel.

"Yes, and if I am being poured out as a drink offering on the sacrifice and service of your faith," Paul continues, after meditating on all of Christ's losses for our sake, "I am glad and rejoice with you all" (Philippians 2:17, NKJV).

Paul's life—his losses and gains both—were poured out as an offering on the altar. His life was not his own. He had been redeemed, bought, rescued from loss, by the Savior, and his work was to redeem the time. His life experiences only counted as gain if they made a difference for Christ—even those experiences that seemed like gain in and of themselves.

Things like growing up with all the advantages of being a good Jewish kid, a direct descendant of Abraham, part of an elite tribe.9 He had the Law on his side, with access to the best scribes and rabbis. He became a Pharisee of Pharisees, zealous and religious to the bone. He was the epitome of what it meant to be Hebrew.

When it came to spirituality, it seemed he had everything.

And then he met Jesus.

It turns out, none of those seeming advantages mattered in the end. "But what things were gain to me, these I have counted loss for Christ," he says. "Yet indeed I also count all things loss for the excellence of the knowledge of Christ Jesus my Lord, for whom I have suffered the loss of all things, and count them as rubbish, that I may gain Christ" (Philippians 3:7-8).

Position, heritage, education, degree—all losses, because they, in the end, could not redeem him. Only Jesus could do that. And you don't have to be Jewish or circumcised, educated or elite, to know Jesus.

Paul counted all his gains as losses so he could gain Christ. Gaining Christ enabled him to count all his losses as gains, down to even death itself: *For me to live is Christ, to die is gain* (Phil. 1:21).

I think what Paul indicates here is complete surrender of his life to Jesus Christ. Circumstances he may have held onto as being important and significant, even if they were good, he released. Let go, opened his hands and his heart to receive the knowledge and presence of Christ. "Everything I once held dear," sings songwriter Brooke Fraser Ligertwood, "I count it all as lost." The chorus of that song goes like this:

Lead me to the cross
Where Your love poured out
Bring me to my knees
Lord, I lay me down
Rid me of myself
I belong to you
Lead me, lead me to the cross[10]

Whatever might be gain in our eyes—marriage, partnership, motherhood, other things—are best left at the cross, where we are overwhelmed and filled with the love and presence of Christ, where He becomes what matters most in all circumstances. The gains of marriage and the gains of singleness, the gains of motherhood or career, education or ministry, count as nothing in comparison to the gain that Jesus brings in both the presence and the absence of those things.

A couple of women in the Bible had that lesson to learn.

She has everything going for her. She is the king's daughter. As the nation's first king, he is respected and successful, and she lives with the benefits of position, privilege, and preference.

She is giddy with love for the handsome, used-to-be shepherd boy who became famous for killing the giant Goliath. Everyone loves him; his name buzzes throughout the nation. Even better, her father favors him as a son-in-law. So he proves himself an even greater hero just to win her, paying double her father's requested bride price: the lives (okay, the foreskins—*ugh*) of two hundred Philistine men. Which makes David that much more attractive to her. He even comes back for her years later, after her father had given her away out of jealousy. What had been lost was restored.

Until the day David, now the king, brings the Ark of the Covenant back to Jerusalem. From a window Michal watches him dancing, twirling, shouting in the street like a madman, full of adoration for God. But Michal isn't thinking about God. She is thinking about the fool her husband is making of himself. Forgetting his position, forsaking his dignity, tossing off his royal robes. She isn't attracted to *that*. And she despises him for it.

All the royalty and privilege gain her nothing as Michal's attitude leads to loss, for she will not have the privilege of bearing the king a son.[11]

She is the best cook in town, the "hostess with the mostess." If anyone has a heart to serve, she does. When it came to putting on a party and laying out a spread, Martha is the person you wanted to have in charge.

And today she is hosting the teacher that many believe is the Messiah. In fact, she herself believes in Him, and she is determined to do her best for Him. She wants it to be so perfect that she keeps trying, unsuccessfully, to get her sister Mary to help her.

But Jesus tells her that Mary—that one who wouldn't set a foot in the kitchen once Jesus arrived—has found the better part, and it would not be taken away from her. All Mary has done that day is sit at His feet, listening.

All the skill and service gain Martha nothing. But Mary gained that which could not be lost.[12]

Gains as losses.

Both Michal and Martha were women who had a lot of advantages, positive things going for them. Things that were surely gifts from God.

Michal had the partnership of marriage to a godly man—the man who was the greatest king in Israel, the man after God's own heart. What wouldn't you or I give to end up with such a man? To partner with him in God's kingdom activities, leading others in godliness and worship?

Yet, as incredible as that kind of marriage partnership must be, it is not the ultimate gain, the thing that completes or finishes us. Jesus does that.

Michal didn't see God as worthy enough, deserving of the kind of passionate praise David lavished upon Him. He wasn't the king of her heart. Only relationship with God could redeem the time through her position and partnership.

Martha, it seems, was single. Yet, she appeared to epitomize the do-it-yourself resourcefulness of the ultra creative woman (think Martha as in Stewart). What's more, she wanted to use all her gifts, her gains, to serve the Lord. Who knows, maybe she had created a new recipe—or a fancy table centerpiece—for Him.

Don't we want to use our gifts and resources for Him as well? As single women, we can host, cook, clean, work, create—all to the glory of God. We can serve in missions and ministries, serve others in our community and in our homes. Yet, that is not the ultimate gain, the thing that completes or finishes us. Jesus does that.

And while Martha served Him, she didn't make Him her first priority, her most important relationship. He wasn't yet the king of her heart. Only relationship with Christ could redeem the time through her talents and service.

Christ over circumstances, good or bad. Even if it means dying to our dreams. Dying to reliance on our good circumstances, gifts, and talents; dying to our longing to receive new, different circumstances. Dying, even, to our ideas of the redemption we know God is going to bring.

Because whatever redemptive circumstance or relationship God gives us, it is not the truest, final gain.

Jesus is.

And He is worthy of the offering we make of ourselves, of our stories. Worthy of us presenting our singleness to Him as a loss He can use as gain. Worthy of us becoming a living sacrifice for Him to pour redemption through.

He is worthy, even if it hurts. And our act of surrender in faith means more to Him than we may ever know.

MORE THAN WE KNOW

All of heaven stands before God, and Satan stands with them. Satan, whose name means Opponent. Hater. Accuser.[13] He had just come in from roaming over the earth, looking to stir up trouble.

Then God says, "Have you noticed Job? Noticed how he follows me, avoids anything and everything that's evil, that's associated with you?"

"Aw, that's only because You protect him," Satan says. "You've given him everything he could possibly want. The man is filthy rich. Loved and happy—he's got it all. But the minute you take away his stuff, he'll curse You. To Your very face!"

It is a dare, a bold dare. All of heaven waits for God's response.

"Okay," God says. "I'll give you power over everything he has. You just can't touch him physically."

Satan vanishes, already hatching a plan. When his hammer strikes, all of heaven is watching to see how Job responds.

All of heaven is watching.

Job has no idea what's going on. No knowledge of the dare, the bet between God and Satan. He's in pain and disbelief. He can't understand what's happening. All he knows is that, suddenly, his story isn't turning out the way he thought it would. But the last verse of chapter one says this: “In all this Job did not sin nor charge God with wrong” (Job 1:22, NKJV).

Soon after, however, Satan stands before the Lord again.

“You incited me against Job,” God says. “To destroy him for no reason. And yet—have you seen him? He’s still an upright man, shunning evil. He’s holding on to his integrity.”

“Skin for skin!” Satan is angry. “Well, he’s still alive, isn’t he? That’s what he’s trying to keep—his life. Strike his body, and You’ll see.”

And God allows Satan to afflict Job, but not to take his life. Once again, all of heaven is watching.

It doesn’t take long for the wretched boils to form, for the incessant itch and agonizing pain to begin. And unfortunately, it doesn’t take long for Job’s wife to say this: “Do you still hold fast to your integrity? Curse God and die!” But Job refuses.[14]

What if he had cursed God? What would have happened in heaven if he had taken her advice?

What wouldn’t have happened on earth was God’s redemptive purpose. Not just His purpose for Job, but His collective purpose for His redeemed people and the broken world they inhabit.

Philip Yancey explains it this way:

> Job teaches that at the moment when faith is hardest and *least* likely, then faith is most needed. His struggle presents a glimpse of what the Bible elsewhere spells out in detail: the remarkable truth that our choices matter, not just to us and our own destiny but, amazingly, to God himself and the universe he rules.

> In short, God has granted to ordinary men and women the dignity of participating in the Great Reversal which will restore the cosmos to its pristine state ... Re-creation involves us; we are, in fact, at the center of his plan... Our very existence announces to the powers in the universe that restoration is under way. Every act of faith by every one of the people of God is like the tolling of a bell, and a faith like Job's reverberates throughout the universe.[15]

There was more going on than Job ever knew. More to be gained through his loss than he could have guessed—gain for the world, and gain for heaven. *Gain for God.*

And for some reason, God chose us to participate in His redemptive gain through our faith. It has been His pattern from the very beginning, at the *protoevangelium*—God's first announcement of coming redemption. He promised at that time to make Woman a vital part of bringing the Redeemer into the world, and His plan all along was to make those He redeemed a part of bringing redemption to those yet unredeemed and to the world itself. It's hard to know why, except that our faith in His redemptive nature brings Him more glory than we comprehend. As Yancey explains it, God lets "his reputation ride on the response of unpredictable human beings."[16]

The redemption that ends up not being all about us or even about other people is, ultimately, all about God. It's about His desire to make Himself known, not just to the nations of the earth, but to the spiritual powers. Known *through us* even in places we can't see while we exercise our faith on earth.

God's nature, known and glorified, is what shouts that He is God. It honors Him as Creator and King, as Sovereign. As the one who overcomes all our unwanted circumstances with His goodness.

Our primary redemptive activity is the fundamental responsibility of every believer: to spread the gospel of Jesus Christ everywhere we go. Millions of people don't give God even a thought, and millions of others believe in every god but the one true God. All of these people desperately need to know a Redeemer lives, that His death and resurrection will save them if they believe. That He will redeem their souls in eternity and their losses on earth.

And there are thousands of those losses on this earth. Countless children and families in third world countries living in extreme poverty. Nations and ethnic groups that have been mistreated and oppressed. Generations of women who have been treated like property, abused, and degraded. Victims of crime, of nature, of human mistakes. My issue of prolonged singleness feels so unimportant in comparison.

But Job's story, and the biblical accounts of God's work in ordinary people's lives, convince me it matters nonetheless. My faith in the midst of my loss, whatever it is, furthers God's redemptive work in the world. It shows others that putting Christ over circumstances makes me a conqueror, not a victim. His goodness and faithfulness to me in my gains and losses—but especially, I think, His redemption of those losses—showcases His grace.

It is His grace, His glorious grace, that He wants to show off, to put on display. That's what Ephesians 1 leads me to believe, anyway. It's all about God's purpose for choosing us as His children, for redeeming us—"to the praise of the glory of His grace, by which He made us accepted in the Beloved" (Eph. 1:6, NKJV).

What the world needs to see is God's grace. Grace, the power that saves and transforms us, that rescues us from loss. Grace, the kindness that envelopes us, the comfort that strengthens us.

And grace, the glory and beauty of the God who loves us, the gentleness that tends to our hearts.

HUSBAND LOVE

It couldn't have been only about Boaz, that love story. I think Ruth needed, desired his love. I think she loved him back, for the love of her first husband Mahlon had been lost—whether or not he had loved her well.

And there's something else. Ruth had never been a mother. All those years of marriage to Mahlon, and no children. The Bible clearly states it was God who enabled Ruth to conceive (Ruth 4:13). Why a child now, with this man? Why this redemption of her previous barrenness that still provided her late husband with an heir? I don't know. Maybe it was simply God's gift to Ruth, another proof that He is the Bridegroom who deeply cares for His Beloved's heart.

In all of God's redemptive activity in our lives, it is our hearts that He is after. He wants us to grow in grace and in the knowledge of Him, to understand His heart, to live in His love. To know what it's like to participate in His redemptive work as a dearly loved and chosen partner.

As we pour our lives like a drink offering on God's altar, we are trusting Him with our heart's unfulfilled dreams. Doing so declares our trust and belief that He alone takes care not only of our souls, but of our hearts. It's what opens us to the experience of His intimate love.

And that is the ultimate redemption of our singleness. The ultimate gain that comes from every moment, day, or season of its losses. It is a reminder that one day we will see Him face to face, and then we will gain the redemption of our souls.

That's what all of our redemptive moments and seasons and life-chapters point to. Being with Him face-to-face is the redemption we ultimately wait for. And He waits for it, too.

NOTES

1. Margaret Becker, *With New Eyes: Fresh Vision for the Soul* (Eugene, OR: Harvest House Publishers, 1998), 18.
2. Robert Morgan, *The Promise* (Nashville: B & H Publishing Group, 2008), 171, 173.
3. Farrar Moore with Sheryl Cook and Betty Plank, *From Hurt to Hope* (Nashville: Caring Resources, 2007), 18.
4. George A. Buttrick, ed., *The Interpreter's Dictionary of the Bible, Volume R-Z* (Nashville: Abingdon Press, 1962), 842.
5. See Genesis 38:6-11.
6. Yitzchak Etshalom, "Analysis of Megillat Ruth (V)," Torah.org, 2005-2007, http://www.torah.org/advanced/mikra/5757/bm/Ruth5.html#.
7. Jack W. Hayford, Litt.D, Note on Ruth 3:10 in the *Spirit-Filled Life Bible*, ed. Jack W. Hayford, Litt.D (Nashville: Thomas Nelson, 1991), 392.
8. Ibid.
9. Jerry Horner, B.A., M.Div., Th.D., Note on Philippians 3:5 in the *Spirit-Filled Life Bible.*
10. Brooke Fraser Ligertwood, "Lead Me to the Cross" on *All of the Above*, compact disc (Hillsong Music Australia, 2007).

11. See 1 Samuel 18:17-27 and 2 Samuel 6:12-13.
12. See Luke 10:38-42.
13. Dick Mills, B.A., D.D., "Word Wealth, Satan" at Job 1:6 in the *Spirit-Filled Life Bible*.
14. See Job 1:1-2:10.
15. Philip Yancey, *Disappointment with God* (Grand Rapids, MI: Zondervan, 1988), 193-194.
16. Ibid., 193.

"And on the hard days, when my stomach fills with lead and tragedy is truly tragedy, I return to the laws of that place: all things work together for the good.
And I consider its time line, time enough to repair. Endless days to bind together that which has been torn apart."

- Margaret Becker[1]

– *Chapter 8* –

ANTICIPATING LIFE *as it was* MEANT TO BE

It is a February morning during my thirty-seventh year, and I walk with Jesus down the streets of my childhood town. Snow falls softly, plentifully, like the tears from my eyes.

My mother died just days ago.

I am desperate for news of her, for her thoughts and doings in her new faraway home with the Lord. *Does she know how we are? Does she even need to know? Oh, Lord! Please hug her for me. Please tell her I love her.*

He is the only link between me and her now. My heart overflows toward Him as I walk, all the questions and emotions, the longing for relationship with her, to somehow have her back.

It is hard to know how to be in the house without her. To know what to do next, how to function. My body and brain operate from habit and routine. And that's why, later that day, I prepare to exercise in the basement. I put on a Chris Tomlin CD that Mom had enjoyed and pick up some weights. Soon, a particularly worshipful and reverent song comes on, an anthem of exaltation to the Lord. The lyrics crescendo toward the chorus:

Blessing and honor
Glory and power

Unto the Lord be praised
Sing with the chorus
Resounding before us
Holy is His name[2]

Suddenly I envision angels and believers worshipping the risen Christ, the Redeemer, in heaven. I feel as if I am standing with them before His throne, as if their present-moment worship were breaking through unseen barriers into my spirit, right in that room. The moment is so amazing I put down the weights and simply stand and sing in His presence.

And in all of this the Lord is answering my prayer, my longing for news of Mom. Instantly I know, I *know*—not in my brain, but in my heart, what she is feeling and doing. She is worshipping and exalting Jesus. She is overjoyed, yet reverent, her face radiant, part of the heavenly chorus. I picture her surrounded by a gigantic congregation, singing with her hands raised toward Him.

And I know that all of her needs are met. Every one. Whatever she needs to know, she knows. She is safe, and she actually sees Jesus, is enveloped in His overpowering love.

In her spirit, she has the fullness of life *as it was meant to be.*

WHAT'S MEANT TO BE

Worship singer Matt Redman has also pictured what it will be like to sing with the choirs of heaven, when all believers stand together, resurrected and glorified, before Him in eternity.

When I stand before your throne
Dressed in glory not my own
What a joy I'll sing of on that day
No more tears or broken dreams
Forgotten is the minor key
Everything as it was meant to be
And we will worship, worship
Forever in your presence we will sing...
An endless hallelujah to the king[3]

Everything as it was meant to be.

What does that really mean for us? It means a day is coming when every need and desire of our hearts will be fully met at all times, every loss fully redeemed. We will receive the eternal salvation that now inhabits our fragile bodies and broken hearts on this fallen planet, and all that's weak and rent and worn will be whole and mended, made completely new.

It means that even this planet will be redeemed, for the culmination of redemption begins when Jesus makes a new heaven and a new earth—essentially recreating the world we currently inhabit. That world will be perfect, Eden restored. Maybe God will even walk through dewy gardens with Man and Woman again.

Paul anticipates this great restoration in Romans 8, presents it as the hope that gets us through the disappointment and hardship of circumstances that weren't meant to be.

> For I consider that the sufferings of this present time are not worthy to be compared with the glory that is to be revealed to

> us. For the anxious longing of the creation waits eagerly for the revealing of the sons of God. For the creation was subjected to futility, not willingly, but because of Him who subjected it, in hope that the creation itself also will be set free from its slavery to corruption into the freedom of the glory of the children of God. For we know that the whole creation groans and suffers the pains of childbirth together until now. And not only this, but also we ourselves, having the first fruits of the Spirit, even we ourselves groan within ourselves, waiting eagerly for our adoption as sons, the redemption of our body. For in hope we have been saved, but hope that is seen is not hope; for who hopes for what he already sees? But if we hope for what we do not see, with perseverance we wait eagerly for it. (Romans 8:18-25, NAS)

Any loss we experience now, Paul says, is a drop in the ocean compared with the glory of what's coming when we receive the redemption of both body and soul. *Glory*, a beautiful word, moonlit-resplendent, sunset-magnificent. *Glory*, an opulent word, a mysterious word, suggesting a yet-hidden fullness to be one day revealed and completely experienced. Like God Himself, and the place He is preparing for us.

All of our redemptive moments and seasons in this life provide just a tiny taste of what we will experience in the life to come. And that is part of their purpose—to whet our appetites. To remind us that earth as we know it is not what we are destined for, that redemptive circumstances and relationships hardly come close to the ultimate redemption they foreshadow.

Randy Alcorn, who has studied the subjects of heaven and eternity extensively, imagines the fullness of that destiny, when we receive our adoption as sons and daughters:

> The most ordinary moment on the New Earth will be greater than the most perfect moments in this life—those experiences you wanted to bottle or hang on to but couldn't. It *can* get better, far better, than this—*and it will.* Life on the New Earth will be like sitting in front of the fire with family and friends, basking in the warmth, laughing uproariously, dreaming of the adventures to come—and then going out and *living* those adventures together. With no fear that life will ever end or that tragedy will descend like a dark cloud. With no fear that dreams will be shattered or relationships broken.[4]

We who know Christ can truly believe the best is yet to come. Not only in relationships with other believers, but with Jesus Himself. In that day, everyone will live in perfect communion and unity with Him. That place of longing, that need for fulfillment, that desire to be known, loved, and accepted, will rest, whole, in His physical presence. No more loneliness and unfulfilled desires, no more disappointment. We will receive the consummate redemption of our souls for which we have long waited.

And Jesus will receive that for which He has long waited, as well—the reward of His sacrifice, the inheritance from His Father. "I will declare the decree: The Lord has said to Me, 'You are My Son, today I have begotten You. Ask of Me, and I will give You the nations for Your inheritance, and the ends of the earth for Your possession'" (Psalm 2:7-8, NKJV).

Jesus will receive *us*. Our redemption is *His* reward. And as He waits, He is preparing a place for us.

AS A BRIDEGROOM WAITS

I sit with others on a golden September afternoon under a flawless sky, facing a horizon lined with bright flaxen trees. Pink and white rose petals are scattered over a grassy aisle between two groups of white chairs. Before long, a lovely bride follows their path toward the luminous horizon, and her smiling groom.

As she approaches him, the groom leaps forward, his gaze fixed upon her face. He takes a few steps, then stops, and waits for the practiced protocol of wedding proceedings. But he can hardly hide his joy.

I think that's how Jesus waits for us, as a bridegroom for his bride, eager with joy and anticipation. The New Testament often uses bridal analogy, husband-and-wife language, to describe the love Jesus has for us. In fact, that's one thing that human marriage is supposed to picture, the kind of intimate, self-sacrificing love between Jesus and the redeemed: "Husbands, love your wives, just as Christ also loved the church and gave Himself for her" (Ephesians 5:25, NKJV).

As a bridegroom waits and prepares for the day when he will be united with his beloved, so does Jesus. Just before His crucifixion,

Jesus told His disciples He was going to the Father and what He would be doing until the day they would be together again. "In my Father's house are many dwelling places, if it were not so, I would have told you; for I go to prepare a place for you. If I go and prepare a place for you, I will come again and receive you to Myself, that where I am, there you may be also" (John 14:2-3, NAS).

Jesus was using wedding language that the disciples would have recognized. In their culture, a woman was legally considered a man's bride during their season of betrothal. During this time, the groom prepared a place for the bride and himself to live, and when his father felt everything was ready, the bridegroom came with great demonstration for the bride. In their book *Falling in Love with Jesus*, Dee Berstin and Kathy Troccoli explain more of the historical background:

> The bride didn't know when the bridegroom would come for her, so she needed to be ready. When he came, the last part of the ceremony was performed, a seven-day celebration including a great wedding feast. It was after this that the bridegroom finally took his bride home.
>
> This makes the picture Jesus paints particularly meaningful. We are betrothed to Him. We are His Bride, but we are in the period of separation. He is preparing a place for us.[5]

Revelation 21 describes the Lamb's wife—the Bride—as a beautiful, gem-covered city. The only ones allowed in and out of that sparkling city are the redeemed that Christ Himself purchased with

His own blood.[6] These are the ones receiving the place that Jesus is now preparing, the ones He waits for as a Bridegroom waits.

In this resplendent city, where the Lamb is the light source, we will be able to see Jesus face-to-face, when we can physically stand in His presence without being destroyed. As we wait for Him to prepare that place, He waits eagerly until the preparations are fully complete. And then He will come as a Bridegroom for His Bride. On that day, our redemption and His inheritance will both be fully received.

Like the eager groom on that September afternoon, Jesus waits with love, joy, and great anticipation. Just as He spent His life on earth serving us, so He serves us now as our High Priest. That work is described in Hebrews 4:14-16: "Seeing then that we have a great High Priest who has passed through the heavens, Jesus the Son of God, let us hold fast our confession. For we do not have a High Priest who cannot sympathize with our weaknesses, but was in all points tempted as we are, yet without sin. Let us therefore come boldly to the throne of grace, that we may obtain mercy and find grace to help in time of need" (NKJV).

He serves us by providing the strength and help we need to live for Him. Paul describes one way He does that: "Who is he that condemns? It is Christ who died, and furthermore is also risen, who is even at the right hand of God, who also makes intercession for us" (Romans 8:34, NKJV).

Jesus actually speaks to the Father on our behalf, as our advocate, at God's right hand. Jesus' work on the cross purchased and redeemed us as His own, and His priestly work of empowerment and intercession continues the renewal of redemption that transforms our present-day lives. Think of it—even now, Jesus is praying for you, for me. It is this work that readies us for the place He is preparing for us.

Our ability and readiness to be with Him is what made the sacrifice worthwhile for Jesus. We are the gain from His loss. And being this gain, *His* gain, is what makes all of our sacrifices worthwhile to us.

THE MOST INTIMATE GAIN

Today she has a headache, the bad ones she sometimes gets. So he does the dishes. Tomorrow she is tired because her heart doesn't function as well as it used to. So he weeds her flower garden, the peonies she so enjoys.

He stoops a little when he stands these days, especially since the heart valve replacement surgery. *Stand up straight*, she urges him as he walks around the living room to exercise. She sits with him during his recent hospital stay, just wants him to be home again.

They tease each other at the dinner table, even lean over for a kiss. They watch TV together in the evenings. They call each other *lover*.

They sit next to each other at his brother's funeral, then her brother's. Their close friend's. And then their daughter's—my mother's.

They are my grandparents. And they have been married for sixty-six years. *Sixty-six years*. Theirs has been a lifetime of intimacy, of becoming one.

A lifetime of intimacy.

That kind of quality marriage is but a picture of the intimate oneness we will have with Jesus someday, as a bridegroom with his bride. When that day comes, we will live an eternal lifetime of unbroken intimacy with Him.

Although marriage is a particular illustration of that intimacy, I count prolonged singleness, with its losses of human partnership and intimacy, as worthwhile because I can gain a deeper, closer relationship with Christ through it. Those moments weeping alone for my mother—His presence surrounds me. Those evenings of restlessness—He listens to me speak what's on my heart. Those life transitions that require such emotional energy for adjustment—He provides strength, comfort and perspective. In all things, He is *always* there to lean on, my very present help. My best friend, confidant, unwavering Love. Though I am single, my personal relationship with Him affords me that taste of what I will have with Him on the eternal day of redemption.

Because He is the ultimate gain from the losses of singleness, the redemption of singleness through His presence on this earth can also point to the thing that marriage points to—becoming one with Christ. All people, whether married or single, can live with Christ as gain in every circumstance. The difference is that married people have a physical experience through human love and sexuality to help them understand a little more how incredible that future unity with Christ will be. And, perhaps, it helps to reveal how deep His desire for us really is.

But that doesn't mean we will have missed out or will have experienced an eternal loss, if we enter heaven having never been married. After all, marriage, and with it, sex, has to have a deeper meaning, has to exist for reasons other than the temporal, if it will not be part of our human experience in heaven—a place where, Jesus said, "they neither marry nor are given in marriage, but are like angels of God in heaven" (Matthew 22:29-30, NKJV).

To me, the sexual intimacy of marriage represents a passion and a desire that goes beyond all physicality. It represents the filling of that deepest soul-and-spirit longing by the deeply passionate love of Christ. I think that's one reason why we so desire marital oneness, and why it was intended by God to be such a wonderful experience. Why, perhaps, writer John Eldredge describes it as immortal.

> There is no union on earth like the consummation of the love between a man and a woman. No other connection reaches as deeply as this oneness was meant to; no other passion is nearly so intense… The passion that spousal love evokes is instinctive, irrational, intense, and dare I say immortal.[7]

Writing about the Ephesians 5 marriage analogy with Christ and the Church, Eldredge continues:

> After creating this stunning portrait of a total union, the man and woman becoming one, God turns the universe on its head when he tells us that this is what *he* is seeking with *us*. In fact, Paul says it is why God created gender and sexuality and marriage—to serve as a living metaphor.[8]

If marriage and sexuality is a metaphor for something else, then it makes sense that it will no longer be necessary, as we currently know it, when the time comes to experience the real thing. And it means that those who have not experienced the metaphor of marriage will receive the redemption of singleness in full through that real thing. Alcorn explains it like this:

> … what we will desire [in heaven]—and always enjoy—is the relational intimacy that was the best part of sex. We may discover, as we look back, that sex prefigured what it means to be lost in intimacy with Christ. Once we're married to him, we'll be at the destination that marital sex pointed to as a signpost… The purpose of sex will have been fulfilled. We'll participate in what sex was always pointing to—deep and engaging relational intimacy. We won't imagine we're missing out.[9]

Dr. Timothy Keller puts it this way:

> Human sexuality is a dim reflection of what it's going to be like to fall into the arms of the Lord on the final day. That's the lover we need. That's the closure we need… If sexuality is such a dim hint of it, and it's such dynamite, what must it be like to finally get the spouse our hearts are looking for?[10]

Whether we are married or single on earth, in heaven we all gain the spouse our hearts are looking for. The best friend, the unconditional acceptance, the ultimate love. True union with Christ is what the signpost of marriage and sexual expression points to.

I can understand in general that the idea of a close marriage relationship on earth will be replaced by the best and closest relationship with Jesus in heaven. But will something replace sex itself? The answer, for me, lies within the purpose and results of sex.

Sexual union is the most private and personal way that two people can get close to one another—as close as it is physically possible to get. It is the most intimate and complete way to know one another in marriage. The King James translation indicates this by saying that a man "knew" his wife when they had sexual intercourse. So, one result of sex is a mutual knowing of one another. Before we meet Jesus in our glorified bodies, we only know Him "in part." As Paul says, "For now we see in a mirror, dimly, but then face to face. Now I know in part, but then I shall know just as I also am known" (I Corinthians 13:12). Jesus knows every detail about us. But when we are unified with Him, we will know, and, I'm sure, keep getting to know, every wonderful, holy and amazing aspect of Him.

Another result of a couple's sexual act of becoming one is a special bond and deep devotion to one another. Speaking on sexuality as it is described in 1 Corinthians 6-7, Dr. Keller says this:

> It is radical self-donation, to give yourself to someone else so deeply that it results in personal transformation and completion. Paul is saying you must never have physical oneness without whole-life oneness. Physical oneness is a bearer and consummation of whole-life oneness... When done the right way, it will result in deep soul nurture, in deep personal transformation and completion...because the physical donation happened in the context of self-donation.[11]

In God's chosen context, sexual oneness completes the whole-life oneness expressed through the covenant of marriage. It demonstrates "radical self-donation" that serves and gives and loves the other person, that results in transformation.

That's what will happen when we stand face-to-face with Christ: We will be transformed. By simply seeing Him, having our bodies already changed from what Paul calls the corruptible to the incorruptible, our spiritual oneness with Him on earth will be consummated into the whole-life oneness that we can never achieve while living in fallen bodies that still battle with the flesh. Nothing on earth can compare with the power and effects of that transformation.

Our worship and devotion to Jesus will be perfected. Completely pure. Undivided. And this is the ultimate gain for Jesus: our uncompromised devotion to Him, the truly selfless love and commitment of a perfect spouse, the obedience and trusting heart of a perfect child.

Two men in the Bible, both devoted lovers of God, seemed to grasp this idea of complete human transformation in the life to come. One is referred to as "the man after God's own heart." The other is called "the disciple whom Jesus loved."

That first man is King David, the father of Christ's earthly, royal ancestry. He thought about the ultimate satisfaction one can achieve on this earth, which, in his mind, was a house full of sons to pass on one's wealth. This, he says, is the only thing "men of the world who have their portion in this life" can look forward to. But David's true gain, his ultimate satisfaction, was elsewhere: "As for me, I will see Your face in righteousness; I shall be satisfied *when I awake in Your likeness*" (Psalm 17:15, NKJV, emphasis added).

The second man is the disciple John, Jesus' closest earthly friend. He thought about the amazing love of God that made us His children. But he didn't stop there, with that reality of life on earth: "Beloved, now we are children of God, and it has not yet been revealed what we shall be, but we know that when He is revealed, *we shall be like Him, for we will see Him as He is*" (1 John 3:2, NKJV, emphasis added).

We have a rather facetious saying about ourselves: "To know me is to love me." Jesus has a truthful saying about Himself: "To see me is to be like me." The transformation that comes from our radical oneness with Christ is *complete conformity to the image of Christ*. The redemption of His untainted image within us, the one we were meant to reflect when He created us. "The ultimate redeeming hunger is to be changed to the glory of his image—to be conformed to his image," writes Calvin Miller.[12]

That image of God will be uniquely expressed through our individual personalities as He always intended. We will still be ourselves—but better. Perfect. Fully redeemed. As Miller continues, "We are never more ourselves and God is never more God than when we enter into union with Christ."[13]

Is this not God's purpose all along, in every circumstance? Pastor Robert Morgan describes God's goal in his book about Romans 8:28:

> Those who love God find themselves agreeing with and attaching themselves to His purpose. The last phrase of the verse says "who are called according to His purpose."

> This is the most difficult part of Romans 8:28 to interpret, and it makes sense only when we go on and read the subsequent sentence in verse 29: "For those He foreknew He also predestined to be conformed to the image of His Son" … God, in His infinite wisdom and intimate care, turns everything that happens to us into tools for good, with a view toward molding us into the image of His Son.
>
> The old word for this, coined by past generations of Christians but now nearly forgotten, is Christlikeness.[14]

It is this fixed purpose of God in every good and bad circumstance that will be fully and finally completed in the day of eternal redemption. And what a continuously perfect experience to anticipate!

GREAT EXPECTATIONS

It is Saturday, the view outside my historic town's Starbucks window like that of a sunny postcard. I watch three boys on the window seat, absorbed in this moment of life. Ten months ago my mother died, and I think about eternity more than ever before.

These boys will die someday. All three of them. Where will they go?

I wonder if they know they were created on purpose, *with* purpose, by a wonderful, redeeming God. And I think about that God, His perspective on my life, on all our lives, so short on earth, so long afterwards.

What am I giving my life to? What am I seeking the most?

The death of someone we love has a way of making us especially aware of life's fleeting fragility, the unknown timing of death's imposition. The meaning and direction of our time on earth. Paul's words in Colossians 3:1-4 hit home:

> If then you were raised with Christ, seek those things which are above, where Christ is, sitting at the right hand of God. Set your mind on things above, not on things on the earth. For you died, and your life is hidden with Christ in God. When Christ who is our life appears, then you also will appear with Him in glory.

All that will last of this earthly life are the things done with and for and in Christ. Circumstances will fade, but His work in and through those circumstances remains. "Circumstances are never eternal; His assignment is always eternal," say my ministry friends Sheryl Cook and Farrar Moore.[15]

Whatever my circumstances, my assignment is to let them make me more like Christ. To see through the eyes of faith that make me more than a conqueror. To have an eternal perspective that allows my life and story to lead others to Him. To know and love and praise and thank Him, all the time. Every day. What if long-lasting singleness is a part of that? What if He wants to use it to prove my faith, my allegiance to Himself? My response to the test makes an eternal difference.

Joseph's God-given dreams, the ones about his brothers bowing down to him, were a test for him: "He sent a man before them, even Joseph, who was sold as a servant. His feet they hurt with fetters; he was laid in chains of iron and his soul entered into the iron, until his word [to his cruel brothers] came true, until the word of the Lord tried and tested him" (Psalm 105:17-19, AMP).

That word was the dream, the one that, for most of Joseph's life, looked like it wasn't going to come true. God used it to test Joseph, and he came through it as a discerning, forgiving, and influential man of God. Because of his character and commitment to God, his earthly life accomplished kingdom purposes, eternal purposes.

It is a sunny spring day, and I sit on the brown leather couch in my counselor's office. In just a couple of weeks, I will celebrate my forty-first birthday. Although I am thinking about my life—the next forty years—with an eternal perspective, right now I'm also thinking about facing another year of singleness. The thought doesn't excite me, even though I've come a long way in processing disappointment.

"Have you ever told the Lord that you'd be okay if you never got married or became a mother?" my counselor asks.

"No," I say, a bit shame-faced. *Not when you put it that way, at least.*

"I think it's time for you to have that conversation," he says.

I know he's right. As soon as I leave his office, I have that conversation. I get into my car and pray passionately and desperately. My deepest desire is to fully surrender my life and dreams to Him, but my emotions don't really match that desire. Even though I speak the words of surrender from a sincere heart, I still feel sad about my marital and motherhood status. *Is that okay?* I wonder. The words of my counselor come back to my mind: "Just ask Him to help you."

So I do. "Please help me, Lord. I trust You and will follow Your ways, even if things don't turn out like I always thought they would," I pray. I realize I haven't fully done the very thing I've written about: let go of the life that hasn't happened so I can take hold of the life He has planned for this season, the life that will lead into my future.

"My dream for my life obviously hasn't worked out, Lord," I say. "Please give me a new dream." I'm not being fatalistic, nor am I feeling resigned. I simply have nothing else to do but humbly place my God-given dreams, broken and all, in His hands. I want to dream His dreams for my life, even if I am not sure right now if I will like them. Maybe that's how Joseph felt when he was hidden away in the dungeon. Maybe, to some degree, that's how Jesus, the Son of Man, felt in the Garden of Gethsemane. Maybe the best possible earthly life that bears the most eternal fruit only comes through the deepest spirit-and-soul surrender.

I finish my prayer. I don't really feel any different, and for the next week, I speak words of surrender every day. Then some family members arrive in town to celebrate my birthday, and my focus turns to time with them.

My turning point season seems to have lasted a long time. Longer, it seems, than those of the women who shared theirs with me. But I no longer feel stuck in disappointment, although it remains there in the background. Instead, I focus on something else: both this present moment and that which transcends it. In this moment, I surrender my singleness to the Lord. In this moment, I thank Him for the wonderful things happening right now. In this moment, I acknowledge God and His plan working something in me that has eternal significance.

Because *for this we have Jesus.*

In Him we have great expectations—yes, for eternity, but also for life on earth. He is the key, the foundation, and the destination for both. In eternity, there will be neither marriage nor singleness. There will be union with Christ, and there will be *family*. We will be part of it. We will fully belong. All loneliness will be abolished, and the family will be fully functional. Life will be perfect. Such an expectation makes a difference in our lives on earth. How are we letting it change us? Who else are we telling about it?

The eternal redemption of singleness lives in our hearts. He is ever present to heal our disappointments and exchange the loss for something good, making us better reflections of Him in the process. God has important work for us to do for Him, a good plan and an eternal purpose for our journey on the way to heaven. It is true even on the most disappointing days when we must walk through a mini turning point to receive hope and comfort and regain God's perspective.

Even recently, I've had to do that. Yet another incredibly young couple—I knew the man when he was an elementary school child—recently got engaged. I had to confess feelings of resentment once again and remind myself what the Lord has been teaching me through my turning point season. I had to hold steadfastly to the things He's spoken.

As I consider how to finish this book, one thing God has spoken to me over and again throughout this journey comes to mind. He's spoken it primarily through His Word and Scriptures I've memorized, and the truth is now real, deep in my heart: God is good. He is merciful and gracious—*abundantly*. Over and over in the Bible, He identifies and describes Himself with these attributes. I see Him differently, freshly, and accurately, standing more in awe of His greatness than ever before. Maybe I've been discovering firsthand something King David knew by experience in every one of his circumstances: "Surely goodness and mercy shall follow me all the days of my life, and I will dwell in the house of the Lord forever" (Psalm 23:6, NKJV).

Because of His goodness and mercy, I am rich in Him. My life is filled with love and redemption, lavished with blessings and provision, brimming with purpose and promise. In my spirit, I know that when His purpose is completed in my singleness, then even that circumstance will change. Of this I am confident, not just for my life, but for yours. In the midst of it, our God is good, always giving grace and glory, the meant-to-be life of Christ shining into every not-meant-to-be circumstance.

Surely goodness and mercy. These two things will fill our lives—*do* fill our lives—on the way to dwelling in His house forever.

Surely.

NOTES

1. Margaret Becker, *With New Eyes: Fresh Vision for the Soul* (Eugene, OR: Harvest House Publishers, 1998), 15.
2. Chris Tomlin, "Exalted (Yahweh)," on *Hello Love*, (sixstepsrecords/Sparrow Records, manufactured by EMI Christian Music Group, 2008).
3. Matt Redman, "Endless Hallelujah," on *10,000 Reasons* (sixstepsrecords/Sparrow Records, manufactured by EMI Christian Music Group, 2011).
4. Randy Alcorn, *Heaven* (Carol Stream, OK: Tyndale House Publishers, 2004), 472.
5. Dee Berstin and Kathy Troccoli, *Falling in Love with Jesus* (Nashville: W Publishing Group, 2000), 70-71.
6. See Revelation 21:2, 9-27.
7. John Eldredge, *The Journey of Desire* (Nashville: Thomas Nelson Publishers, 2000), 129.
8. Ibid., 130.
9. Alcorn, *Heaven*, 353.
10. Timothy Keller, "Sexuality and Christian Hope," April 18, 2004, MP3 audio file, http://sermons2.redeemer.com/sermons/sexuality-and-christian-hope.
11. Ibid.
12. Calvin Miller, *Into the Depths of God* (Bloomington: Bethany House Publishers, 2000), 120.
13. Ibid., 107.
14. Robert Morgan, *The Promise* (Nashville: B & H Publishing Group, 2008), 84-85.
15. Farrar Moore with Sheryl Cook and Betty Plank, *From Hurt to Hope* (Nashville: Caring Resources, 2007), 74.

Acknowledgments

Thank you, Sheryl, for hearing my story, reading my book, and cheering me on. You are truly an inspiration.

Thank you to all the single and previously single women who shared your stories, insights, breakthroughs, and tears with me. It is a privilege to be trusted with even a little piece of your hearts. Thank you for allowing me to share parts of your stories with others. You are a blessing.

Thank you to all those who listened to my book ideas over the years, read early manuscripts, provided feedback, and offered encouragement. Thank you to Pastor Dale for your teaching of the Word that helped me better understand who I am in Christ. I would not be who I am today without your input.

Thank you, Ashley Hagan and Joshua Sandefur for your camaraderie and partnership as Inkwell writers and for helping me move forward.

Thank you, Jesus, for loving me as a perfect Bridegroom loves His Bride and for being my Redeemer.

Finally, thank you, Daniel, for being more than worth the wait. In you God has brought me the redemption of singleness.

CPSIA information can be obtained
at www.ICGtesting.com
Printed in the USA
LVHW05s1336010918
588601LV00002B/3/P

9 780692 072592